Dedication

I dedicate this book to my wonderful wife Patricia; our three wonderful children Brian, Mike and Katie; and our friendly friends—Ben our very happy dog, who recently became an Angel, and Buddy, our always cheerful cat.

Thank You All!

Acknowledgments

I appreciate all the help that I have received in putting this book together as well as all of my other 135 other published books.

My printed acknowledgments had become so large that book readers "complained" about going through too many pages to get to page one of the text.

And, so to permit me more flexibility, I put my acknowledgment list online, and it continues to grow. Believe it or not, it once cost about a dollar more to print each book.

Thank you and God bless you all for your help.

Please check out www.letsgopublish.com to read the latest version of my heartfelt acknowledgments updated for this book. FYI, Wily Ky Eyely loves this book and recommends it to all. Click the bottom of the Main menu!

Thank you all!

Preface:

Brian W. Kelly enjoyed putting this book together. Being the author of each of the ten books, which outline the major solutions for the severe domestic ills afflicting America today, made it easy for Brian to pick and choose the synopses that would be in this Whitman's Sampler / CliffsNotes version.

Brian's objective was to put in one condensed book the many solutions that have evaded the best of the best in Congress and the presidency for many years for one reason or another. Brian believes he did the job for Congress if we can get them to read the book. A secondary objective for Kelly was that he hoped that when any of the "CliffsNotes" versions were read, the reader would believe they had gotten the full picture of both the problem and the solution, even though the Whitman's Sampler synopsis would not contain all of the supporting detail.

Kelly is very happy that he was able to achieve both objectives.

Why did Brian W. Kelly write this book?

Brian W. Kelly saw the problems with millennials and the problem with the negative influences of coffee breath college professors on America while he served as a college professor himself. Kelly cares about America, millennials, those affected by foreigners poaching in America, and American taxpayers who are carrying the big burden of supporting those who choose not to chip-in.

Brian loves America and like President Trump, he wants America to be great because great Americans, who are permitted to live without government constraints, are the vehicle which will make America and all Americans great again.

You will love this book because the major domestic problems that America faces are solved within the short Whitman's Sampler / CliffsNotes versions of the detailed solutions.

Thank you for being so nice as to purchase this book and for helping keep America the only place in the living world where freedom matters more than anything else.

I wish you the best.

Brian P. Kelly, Publisher
Wilkes-Barre, Pennsylvania

Table of Contents:

About the Author

Brian W. Kelly retired as an Assistant Professor in the Business Information Technology (BIT) program at Marywood University, where he also served as the IBM i and Midrange Systems Technical Advisor to the IT Faculty. Kelly designed, developed, and taught many college and professional courses. He continues as a contributing technical editor to a number of IT industry magazines, including "The Four Hundred" and "Four Hundred Guru," published by IT Jungle.

Kelly is a former IBM Senior Systems Engineer and IBM Mid Atlantic Area Specialist. His specialty was designing applications for customers as well as implementing advanced IBM operating systems and software facilities on their machines.

He has an active information technology consultancy. He is the author of 146 books and numerous technical articles. Kelly has been a frequent speaker at COMMON, IBM conferences, and other technical conferences.

Brian was a candidate for US Congress from Pennsylvania in 2010 and he brings a lot of experience to his writing endeavors. Brian Kelly knows how to solve most of the domestic problems in the US. Let's hope the Congress hears him out.

Chapter 1 Great Domestic Solutions Ready for 2018

The chapter was written by Brian Patrick Kelly, the author's oldest son, to help kickoff this memorable book. Enjoy!

Writing books can be fun

Prolific author Brian Kelly produces so many books in a given year even his family cannot explain how he does it. His most popular books throughout the years, such as Great Moments in Alabama Football, have focused primarily on sports themes, but that is not his original claim to fame. Kelly's initial prior experience was problem solving in information technology and later political diagnosis and remedies. His U.S. domestic policy recommendations are second to none.

Anyone in the patriotic or conservative world who finds themselves flirting with finding an innovative solution to the domestic ills that have been eluding supposed experts for far too long will find their needs more than satisfied by one of Kelly's refreshing works. For open minded liberals or progressives, many of his answers can be hung on either side of the aisle.

Kelly's solutions are deceptively simple and occasionally counterintuitive at first glance. One's first question may be, "Can something so simple actually solve the problem?" After reading further and understanding his proposals, Kelly aspires to allow a new world of thought to unfold before the eyes and instill the positive belief that many of the nation's seemingly intractable maladies are indeed curable.

Historically, great thinkers and influential problem solvers possess an uncanny ability to translate otherwise arduous complex notions into language that any audience can readily understand. Kelly prides himself on cutting through argument, debate and doubt, and offers solutions that all can process and appreciate. Brian's plain talk solutions are authentic, cogent, clear, and palpable, quite unlike rocket science. He reveals a logical path for readers that culminate in "Of course!" rather than "What?!"

Brian has been quietly solving domestic problems for many years with various iterations of books that in 2017 have all been fine-tuned to meet the needs of today. Even his early books, such as No Taxation Without Representation, were considered groundbreaking. The 2017 editions of all of Kelly's books written to solve America's most urgent domestic issues are his most refined yet.

His readers are continually amazed that a layman who spent his life as a technician for IBM could redeploy his analytical and problem-solving skills to the broader challenges facing America. He has accomplished this repeatedly and in 2017, he has done it again by preparing the fixes that the Congress and the President can deploy in 2018.

With this book of synopses, Brian Kelly now has one hundred and forty-six books to his credit. They vividly describe various aspects of American life. A good many of Kelly's 2017 books specify how the nation can address its many challenges in the current century.

While Kelly may allocate personal time to offering advice on issues like how many crossing guards are needed at a local intersection in Wilkes-Barre, Pennsylvania, he does not purport to be an expert on such matters which he has not yet studied in depth. By contrast, Kelly has spent years contemplating the major social and domestic problems in the United States and finds himself peerless in his insight.

To remain adept, Kelly perpetually studies the major domestic issues of our time and examines and reexamines potential sensible solutions. He ran for U.S. Congress as a Democrat in 2010, adhering to his vow to take no campaign donations in 2010 and was pleased to receive 17% of the vote despite being vastly outspent and having little prior name recognition.

He understood the system to be rigged against ordinary Americans like himself who are not indentured to a major donor with plenty of reserve funds and harbored no illusions of overnight success. Kelly is not for purchase; his merit lies in diagnosis and rectification of problems.

Increasingly, more Democrats such as Brian are beginning to realize that the entrenched class, also known as "the Swamp," has control over everything consequential in the U.S. except for the often-misdirected voting power of the people. Though we still retain control of the government to some extent, we often fail to correctly exercise our power. Kelly believes that even the few crumbs and inches gained are only acquired once those gains have been predetermined by the powers to be worthless. Like many of you, he opposes our domination by this Swamp.

Like Donald Trump, your author wants to make America great again. Not being president of course, makes it a lot more difficult to insert real solutions into the political mix of today. Brian Kelly is your average normal guy but for one difference. In his role as the most published non-fiction author in America, Kelly has built a solution for each of the most pressing domestic US issues of today.

For each problem, Kelly has at least one book in his arsenal that solves the problem. Sometimes it takes two and sometimes even more than two books to completely solve the most nagging issues.

Brian Kelly writes, and he writes, and he thinks, and he articulates. But, as a normal, regular American; he has no power or resources to force his ideas upon anyone. It is not an easy task.

Even Donald Trump as CEO of America is having problems dislodging the gunk and muck in the Swamp and getting his agenda implemented. The Swamp dwellers have lots of spare cash to fight all comers. The Establishment has many people to whom they pay large sums to fight for them every day. For that, the political junkies in the SWAMP get the best advice about how to keep the President at bay.

Brian Kelly's major domestic solutions are contained in his books. Ten books unfortunately to solve ten major problems provides a lot of material for solutions. Consequently, it is too much reading all at once for even the best of us. And, so, the purpose of this "Whitman's Sampler" book of synopses, is to be a book of books, written in "CliffsNotes" style for easy reading and comprehending.

The book is titled: *Top Ten American Political Books for 2018*. It provides a comprehensive set of summaries on the best approaches to tackle the major domestic US issues that we are facing in 2018. It is designed to be read one chapter at a time in a short period so that Americans can have a big win for the country. When the right people read this set of "CliffsNotes" books and begin to pass laws and implement the plans contained herein, America will be well on its way to greatness again, working to achieve independence from those keeping us down.

Brian Kelly is not a total cynic but a realist like many lifelong Democrats whose disgust with established special interests has made them gravitate towards the countermeasure of Donald Trump. Why should ordinary people volunteer to be pushed around by dishonest Democrats anymore? Despite being a billionaire, Trump relates to the people in a way that breaks through the authoritarian forced politeness behind which masquerades the nefarious interests of the entrenched political class.

Donald Trump takes no salary as he finds being a great president as reward enough for his daily toil. Even as he is constantly assailed by our disingenuous and certifiably fake news media, he dusts himself off and goes right back at it the next day on behalf of all of us.

Democrats have failed their original vision of a world where families can earn a decent wage by working, opting instead to reward their anti-American donors who prey on the very people the Party was founded to help prosper. Democrats want the people to believe that their captured government should be sufficient for the people's needs, having done their best to extinguish any members who otherwise would be driven to work on behalf of the population at large.

One of the greatest challenges President Trump faces is how to rehabilitate faith in our system, when the Democratic Party, a once reliable bedrock institution, is now bitterly distrusted. We all wish him well on that account.

So, what does someone without Mr. Trump's resources do? Most of us cannot afford to run a successful campaign but are united in our goal of *Making America Great Again*. Kelly hopes his ideas can influence the nation and President Trump personally, as though they both lack pure omniscience, they share a powerful intellect, heart of gold, and desire to restore America to its former glory.

Kelly has some great ideas. He increasingly sells more and more books each month but because he currently lacks fame, his solutions have yet to reach a widespread audience that could one day promote the policies that ultimately reach the President's desk. He writes, thinks, and articulates, knowing full well that his ideas' path to fruition is an indirect one. While Mr. Trump has the power and influence to accomplish many of his plans for the nation, Brian understands that his ideas are going nowhere unless they are put into action prompted by popular will and executed by the President's pen.

As noted previously, the road ahead is difficult. Even Donald Trump himself is having problems dislodging the sludge and serpentine slugs in the dreaded swamp who have full control of America. They are able to spare any expense to protect their system of chicanery at all costs, including paid lackeys in the media who defend the indefensible.

They are well organized and protected. Another lever in the system of revolving doors include the overpaid consultants who provide inside access to electoral success. For many of the most venal knaves in office purporting to be public servants, re-election of course is a vanity success for its own sake, rather than enabling a better life for the citizens of this country.

So, what does Brian Kelly have to offer? This book provides a good overview. Titled *Top Ten American Political Books for 2018*, it is a synopsis on the best approaches to tackle domestic US issues in 2018 for Americans to finally achieve success in the country.

Nothing in life worth having is easy and the only thing once can do alone in life is fail. And, so, Brian Kelly has had a good friend for the last six years, Congressman Lou Barletta who also hails from Northeastern Pennsylvania and currently serves as its representative. Kelly and Barletta became friends when Kelly ran for Congress, lost in the primary, and asked Barletta how he could help him win his Congressional seat.

Kelly continually communicates with and meets with the Congressman to discuss his ideas for the improvement America. The Congressman is always warm and engaging and Kelly hopes to demonstrate enough popular political will to move forward with his policy ideas. Kelly believes the Congressman is the real deal, so to speak, so he continues to raise awareness of these issues in his presence as he believes it to be one of the best avenues to reach President Trump.

Brian supports this Congressman in 2018 for his next big strategic operation—a run for the US Senate. Pennsylvania currently has one of the most inept Senators representing the state in Pennsylvania history. Bob Casey Jr. a nice enough guy from Scranton, is regarded as but a shadow of the towering figure his father was, when the senior Casey served as Governor of Pennsylvania.

Most people in the local area gave up hope on Casey Jr. a long time ago, as he revealed himself to be little more than a water-carrier for Barack Obama and then Hillary Clinton in her notoriously corrupt failed bid for President in 2016.

To put Casey in perspective, when he first ran for the U.S. Senate, a Philadelphia Inquirer columnist wrote that Casey's *make-no-waves style* was as exciting as "oatmeal." Considering the Inquirer's center-left editorial bias, the fact that this was the most positive thing they could muster was a surprise to even Democrats.

Brian Kelly wrote this new compendium book so that between the covers of just one book, he is now able to introduce the precepts that are detailed in all ten books released in 2017. In this way, policy makers and interested citizens alike can have an even more concise tool from which to create the legislation necessary to disinfect the United States of the major issues that are keeping the country from moving forward without impediment.

By way of a list, as a topical introduction, these are the major domestic issues for which Brian Kelly has fashioned the most appropriate solutions for 2008.

- ✓ Saving millennials so they do not become the lost generation
- ✓ Refranchise student borrowers
- ✓ Prescribes how colleges and universities can become more honest in promising the world to 17-year-old high school kids, and locking them in to huge debt
- ✓ Remove welfare as a free lunch
- ✓ Ending healthcare redistribution
- ✓ Provide Social Security recipients with a COLA that makes up for past inaccuracies
- ✓ Provide a no-amnesty, no cost, pro-American rescue of illegal aliens from the shadows.
- ✓ Provide cash for self-deportation of illegal aliens
- ✓ Provide cash for self-deportation of anchor babies
- ✓ Provide cash for self-deportation of two-term green card holders.
- ✓ Provide no amnesty; no way!
- ✓ Provide a system so that Americans have first opportunities for every job that comes available.
- ✓ Save well over $500 billion per year on immigration costs
- ✓ Repeal Obamacare with a market, not a government replacement.
- ✓ Downsize the EPA by 95%
- ✓ Avoid Taxation Without Representation

The solutions written in the latter part of 2017 are contained in Brian Kelly's ten books that are outlined in this book titled, *Top Ten American Political Books for 2018* and the solutions are primed to help America with its domestic problem set for 2018.   The books are listed in reverse order of publishing date. The book titles contain solutions for tall of the above listed problems.

The Top Ten Political Books in America for 2018 are as follows:

- Taxation Without Representation Fourth Edition--Can the U.S. Avoid Another "Boston Tea Party?"

- DELETE the EPA! EPA agenda is not to save human lives. Is its insidious goal world population control?
- Deport All Millennials Now! It ought to be easy. They'll line up like it's a free vacation
- No Free Lunch—Pay Back Welfare   The first book that recommends that welfare should not be free money
- Wipe Out All Student Debt Now! Unique solutions to the $1.45 Trillion debt accumulation
- Boost Social Security Now!   A solution to get Seniors out of the poorhouse; Hey buddy, can you spare a dime?
- Legalizing Illegal Aliens Via Resident Visas-- A great Americans-first plan which saves $Trillions. Learn how!
- Pay-To-Go-- An America-first immigration fix   No more deportations
- Obamacare: A One-Line Repeal   Congress must get this done
- 60 Million Illegals in America!!! A simple, America-first solution!

Thank you,
Brian Patrick Kelly
Editor in Chief & Publisher of Lets Go Publish! Publishers.

Chapter 2 Taxation Without Representation Fourth Edition

BRIAN W. KELLY

TAXATION WITHOUT REPRESENTATION

Can the U.S. Avoid Another "Boston Tea Party?"

Fourth Edition

Contains full text of the following:
Articles of Association,
Declaration of Rights and Grievances,
Declaration of Independence,
Articles of Confederation,
U.S. Constitution Bill of Rights
& the 27 Amendments

Can the U.S. Avoid Another "Boston Tea Party?"

Book purpose:

The purpose of this book is to remind *"We the People,"* to be vigilant about electing knaves, who claim to be "honorable," to the highest offices of our national government. Yet, the book acknowledges that *"We the People"* too often get sucked in for many reasons and wind up with representatives who care little about us or the country. The book prescribes a solution for those who love America to be able to stop all this in its tracks and return our glorious America to its former days of glory—when honor was earned and bestowed only upon the honorable.

The story in the book

This book relies on the Constitution, the founding documents, Articles of Association, Declaration of Rights and Grievances, Declaration of Independence, and the Bill of Rights.

Taxation without Representation unearths and explores a massive dilemma for U.S. Citizens. The US began without representation. Then, the Colonies fought a war of independence to acquire representation. Now, our beloved representatives have fallen for the candy-coated wiles of the new kids on the block--obscenely rich mega-corporations and members of the establishment of both parties.

This book offers a walk-though about how our government once was, how it improved, and how it again eroded and regressed from freedom to a new set of oppressive roots. The book highlights the major issues affecting the American worker, particularly the wholesale exportation of jobs to legal and illegal foreign nationals.

The book also discusses how both political parties are preventing independent candidates from appearing on ballots and the problems presented by voting machines surreptitiously designed with technology that enables an interested party's surrogates to manipulate and even override the people's choices.

Our representative democratic republic is definitely in trouble. We have the biggest bumbling set of idiots ever who supposedly are representing us, while scobbing-up every perquisite possible for themselves. While pointing out definitively that we pay too much in taxes, this book also offers a number of unique solutions to help get us back on a track of which the founders would smile. You will too. Enjoy!

Table of Contents

Preface:

Brian W. Kelly wrote this book because our representatives in the House, the Senate, in state legislatures and city councils have forgotten their duties as representatives of the people.
Additionally, the president, the governors, the mayors, and other prefects of the people in the executive branches of governments across the land have conveniently forgotten that the primary

fundamentals of our representative constitutional democracy (republic) start with representation.

"No taxation without representation" was the catch phrase in the period of 1763-1776 to summarize the major grievances of the American colonists in the Thirteen American Colonies, incipient kernels of what would later become the United States of America.

When King George III of England and the English Parliament began to impose new taxes on the colonists (Stamp Act, Intolerable Acts, etc.) without their concurrence, Reverend Jonathan Mayhew of Boston coined this term during one of his sermons in Boston.

Another Bostonian, a politician by the speak of the day, James Otis, changed this just a bit and he is well known for the phrase, "taxation without representation is tyranny." Tyranny it was and in this book, you will see that tyranny it surely is again.

In 1773, American colonists violently opposed the tax on tea imports at the most celebrated Tea Party of all time. The Boston Tea Party is recognized as the first experience in which the colonists acted against the Crown. Of course, the British could not accept this "illegal act" as they saw that it would undermine the authority of the Crown and Parliament.

When the British Government began to crack down on these "illegal activities" performed by the colonists, the colonists chose to defend themselves in case the British Government did not hear their sincere pleas to correct the abuses.

Though today the tea still may be contained safely in the ships in Boston Harbor, millions have expressed discontent of the US government just several years ago by holding their own tea parties all over the US in protests against the American government. Bernie Sanders and Donald Trump have awakened the same spirit of "NO" today to a government that thinks it owns the people of this great country. Donald Trump is now President of our great country. Bernie Sanders struck a chord with young votes because of his sincerity and his honesty.

Beware the lulling idea that your government cannot be taken over by rich members of a ruling class, or de-facto by corporations, or even by a powerful president with disdain for capitalism. Look how close former President Obama came to destroying America. The quickest way to assure this can happen in our time is to stop paying attention; stop caring; and stop voting and to let them simply have their way.

Brian W. Kelly wrote this book because he cares, and I am publishing this book because I care. Together, BWK and I hope to energize Americans again in the still new millennium as in the 1700's. Our mantra is that this magnificent democracy, for which much blood was shed, continues to be worth fighting for.

I hope you enjoy reading this book and that you will remain vigilant and take the actions necessary so that this experiment in democracy, this United States of America, can persevere and succeed for many hundreds and hundreds of more years.

For now, I wish you the best! Yes, we suffer from Taxation without Representation but as we awaken to that reality, we can make it much better by paying attention to who we make our elected representatives.

Sincerely

Brian P. Kelly, Editor & Publisher

Ch 1 America Gained and Lost Its Independence
No excerpts are taken for this synopsis from Ch 1.

Ch 2 We Elect Talking Heads & Empty Suits

When the following thought marched into my mind only a few short years ago, "America is a representative democracy," I began to ask myself, isn't it time that we actually had some real "representation" from our so-called representative government? The way it now works provides far too much separation between us, the electors, and them, the elected officials coordinating our pooled resources for the alleged benefit of "everyone." But who is everyone? A genuinely compelling concern for our government or a Disney-like utopian myth?

I propose the latter. Our government is wholly unaccountable. Our lawmakers have no trouble going with the flow and committing us to years of debt without even taking the time to read the legislation for which they vote. Even worse, its members, allegedly our civil servants, do not even seem to care for our own wellbeing. They care for their leadership and themselves, but they just can't get it into their heads that we the people count at all.

While running for office, it seems that incumbent and aspiring prospective officials saturate our consciousness day-in and day-out, wheedling us into their self-perpetuating power games with promises of responsiveness, unity, and even candor. Yet, even then, only one primary concern lurks on their minds, that sine qua non of their very daily existence, the next election.

A forthcoming election could be as distant as two years and still your impending loss of job, perhaps due to a plant relocating to China, or one closing in Michigan, is at best a secondary afterthought to the very men and women promising you change, when you want it, and stability, again when they believe you want it.

Unfortunately, their priorities are one dimensional and your job going to China or just no longer existing, isn't the focus. Eventually they get re-elected by us, and go off to Washington for yet another term. The cycle starts again with the eternal candidate alternating between Washington and their well-insulated, gated communities far enough from the common people that they don't have to care what you think.

It's Never Them

When they are about to raise your taxes, they are particularly inconspicuous. Being numbed to the excesses and decadent corruption of everyday politics, you may not expect communication and straight answers and, so you are not disappointed. You hear about the tax issues on TV or in the paper, not from your elected because your opinion on the matter really doesn't matter. They would rather converse via cellular or Blackberry or iPhones with some of the only entities who truly can garner their attention—co-Congressmen, the affluent, the corrupt media, and of course, major campaign donors.

Discussing an important issue with you, while seeming like a charming noble way for a representative to spend an afternoon, is discarded as wanton. It's dismissed simply because it would not tangibly benefit anyone's reelection campaign which, as we have all learned, begins the day oaths of office are sworn.

They want us to think that any tax increase is caused by imaginary rival agents or economic forces beyond their control. They will convey this to us with the sole purpose of acquiring our hard-earned money. Apparently, they promise, any burdens will fall on some imaginary "other person" and we will remain unscathed.

Horrifically but as expected though, when we get our tax bills from the bureaucracy, we find out that we were that "other" person. Since the bureaucracy sent us the bill, we blame the bureaucracy, and again we let our politicians off the hook, just like our "representative" hoped we would. And again, they live to run for another election, their only professional motivation in life.

Talk to the Hand

Most individuals feel that their needs and opinions are not taken very seriously by elected representatives who occupy the hallowed chambers of our government buildings. We would call it a communication break-down but there really is no communication.

Despite our inability to get legislators to know our side of important issues, such as taxation, jobs, illegal aliens, etc., and more recently, bailouts, and healthcare, we treat them with too much respect. We intrinsically know that they care only about the desires and opinions of pressure groups, lobbyists, corporate executives and owners, as well as the plain old rich.

Only these voices reach our representatives. Yet, time and time again, we let them off the hook. Politicians cut themselves off from their electorate by choice to be spared from accountability.

Yet, whenever necessary, they make a resurfacing experience and always in time for the next election. Why are we so nice to them?

You may not see them in action when they work the halls of Congress, but you do see them work the wedding halls when it is the height of the election season. In Congress, the typical representative appears to have some sort of godly mandate, on the basis of which, whatever they put forward must be good for everybody.

However, whether it is a good idea or not, and they rarely are, you know the idea more than likely came from the whispers of the chosen elite. Politicians do not serve most of their electorate and they get away with it because again, we do not hold them accountable, and we do not break their pattern by showing up on their doorsteps with our needs.

It's time to fire them—every one of them!

What would happen to the placid world of the politician if its constituency took them to task? What might happen to these politicos if the citizens suddenly became extremely active? How would the elected representative handle such a massive increase in constituent contact? Would they become beneficent and magnanimous? Or would they choose the hermitage approach and lock the gates and doors and hope the rabble will go away?

Especially if we think they would never put up with our entreaties, we should deluge them anyway and help power our representative democracy back to working order. In our hearts, we know we would see nothing more than congressional aides coming out of the woodwork to "see if they can help matters." That of course is code for "see if they can shut us up!" And, for their lack of efforts on our behalf, we should do the only humane thing: fire them! Throw the bums out. They've had their day.

Regular people are taking notice

There is a clear and fundamental problem with our government, even when we are on different sides of most of the other issues. In

Mitt Romney's campaign, he said that Washington was "broken."
With Obama right before Trump, it may be just "broke."

Either way, it is almost beyond repair. For the broken
government that gave us the infamous Bush Dubai Ports deal,
whose ex-Presidents represent foreign nations, and who have
passed laws such as the "uniform labeling of products" fiasco, a
fellow citizen of mine, Rik Reppe, a regular guy and self-described
performer, writer, raconteur, and occasional business geek, ripped
the establishment a new item in his blog at the URL below.

http://reppe.blogs.com/reppecom/2006/03/because_we_get_.html

Reppe believes that we the people get exactly what we deserve
because we elect these talking heads and empty suits, who owe
their allegiance to some corporation someplace. To demonstrate
the rage that is out there in cyberspace about what an absolutely
abysmal bunch of political louts run our government, I picked two
paragraphs from Rik's rants on the labeling topic. Though many
things have been former president Obama's fault for eight long
years, even more as days go by, lack of representation is not a
recent phenomenon. These caught Rik's ire, for example, back,
pre-Obama, in March, 2006

"But why should we believe the House of Representatives is
looking out for us and not sucking at the corporate t...t? That's
easy. You know the House has got your back...you know they're
grandstanding for votes...on any and all issues on which no public
hearings are held. Because we all know that politicians who are
looking out for the people hate it when those efforts are brought to
the attention of the people. Hate it, hate it, hate it. The last
thing...the very last thing in the whole wide political universe any
politician wants to do in an election year is to trumpet efforts to
help the voters thus securing easy camera and soundbite time.
...
And ain't it grand that on the same day the Senate passed a
completely impotent and toothless "lobbying reform" bill that
contains no actual provision to enforce the increased disclosure
the impotent and toothless product of their collective minds
created (passed by a vote of 90-8 proving that as much as I want
this to be a Republican issue it f...ing well isn't) it takes up an issue
that had been voted down by every Congress since 1994 and is
only back to the influence of lobbyists? You may hate what our

Senators are doing but you gotta love that kind of brazen chutzpa, don't you?"

Ch 3 We Get the Government We Deserve

Sometimes it seems that the gift of reelection that we give to our undeserving representatives makes them feel independent of "We the People."

Do they work for somebody else?

The chasm between electors and the elected is widening as we speak. The John Does and the Jane Q. Publics have lost faith in their representatives. Many have become fully disinterested in the political process, though the healthcare "debate" and the fresh air at the "Town Meetings" may be just the cure for this malaise.

For some time, with good reason, the public has felt disenfranchised from the basic right of a citizen to participate in their democracy. Some may handle this by ignoring politics. Others may find alternative ways to attempt to influence the course of events, sometimes through friends and associates, but not always with very positive results.

Sometimes as we have seen in our history, the frustration of humans in our democracy leads to violence as in the civil rights movements and the anti-war rallies of the 1960's and the riots in Los Angeles in the 1990's. Are we there again? Perhaps the main reason that the system even seems to work is that constituents do not make many demands -- at least till now, and like Reppe says,

"We Get the Government We Deserve."

This is the root cause that permits politicians, masquerading as our representatives, to represent others' interests. It is an understatement to suggest that representatives are out of touch with the will of the people. Even the newly elected begin to share the wealth of their constituency with others as they begin their "service." They have this need to redistribute income and now they are redistributing healthcare.

The Brave New World

Note: http://en.wikipedia.org/wiki/Brave_New_World,

Aldous Huxley wrote the <u>Brave New World</u> as a novel in 1932. The book is about the future and its setting is London, 2540 A.D. The novel anticipates that all of the reproductive advancements that today are just notions in a lab someplace, including biological engineering, and sleep-learning, will be commonplace in the future and will be used to change society.

The book talks about drug use as pacifiers to make the people feel better and loudspeakers used to get across the message.   Later Huxley wrote two other books on the topic, one thirty years later in which he saw the future coming much sooner and the other, The Island, which took the sterile notions of Brave New World and made them more attractive and more positive. For example, loudspeakers were replaced by pleasing parrots trained to offer uplifting slogans to the unsuspecting people.

Is our current day, " the Brave New World revisited," is a new deal in which the Government hands out pacifiers to keep the citizenry in a state of euphoria? What does such euphoria look like...???

Maybe most people do not want to know. You'll have to find the book to find out more. I hope that I piqued your interest in the idea of paying attention to the deeds politicians do!

Chapter 3 Delete the EPA

DELETE
the
EPA

*The EPA agenda is not
to save human lives...*
Is its insidious goal world population control?

BRIAN W. KELLY

The EPA agenda is not to save human lives. Is its insidious goal world population control?

Book Purpose:

Would that not be a terrible idea that we Americans may have been letting others die of disease because our own EPA was OK with that notion. Is the EPA an agent of the liberal notion of population control? I am so pleased that former president Barack Hussein Obama no longer controls such a powerful agency.

Preface:

This is the third edition (2018) of the very popular book, Kill the EPA! It is timeless, but we have updated it to make it even more timeless. This time we released it with a new title, *DELETE the EPA.*

The book has already been read by thousands and thousands of Americans who want a nice environment but do not want a rogue agency, the EPA helping to destroy our country.

Nothing stands still in time including the EPA, though it surely should. Ralph Kramden ought to send it to the moon. This "third" edition is refreshed and updated and easier to read. Some inconsequential material stuff has been purged. However, the still outrageous stories about how the EPA, a killer agency, trying to preserve itself are still in here.

As the EPA has promised, people all over the world will be able to live their lives to completion, but the little lie the EPA does not ell by omission is that people may die a little or a lot sooner if it were up to them to save the environment.

The original book was written under Barack H. Obama's watch. Many believe still that he was watching closely only so that he could destroy America using his EPA as a primary tool. He used his pen and his phone to get a lot done but then Mr. & Mrs. Potato Head, Mighty Mouse, and Superman came to the rescue to save the day for plants, animals and, according to the EPA, the least of all critters, humans, Now Mr. Obama is gone and even the plants are rejoicing.

Like Paladin, San Francisco, Our new President, Donald J. Trump does not bring out his big weapons unless he has to do so. When brought out, like Paladin, Trump uses them 100% of the time.

President Trump has no fear because what he is doing is for the good of America. He makes most Americans feel good about being American. Thank you, Mr. President.

As you read this book, and you ask how we can best help America to be saved; think of these two choices. In our future, we have just these choices: 1 "DELETE the EPA from the world," or (2) Bring on the Donald and "Fire the EPA!" Either choice works for me.

I hope you enjoy this book and I hope that it inspires you to take action to help change the members of Congress who choose to defy the American Constitution. If need be, replace every member of Congress and the Senate (up for reelection) unless we can find verifiable statements that they are not responsible for perpetrations against the people.

The big job now is to replace Congress, as the people have already elected a great new president for the next seven years. Our new President, Donald J. Trump loves America and wants America to succeed. He is already making America a better country. With a stroke of the new President's Pen, and a little cooperation from a lame Congress, we can all say Bye Bye EPA! Won't that be nice?

I wish you the best

Brian Kelly

Table of Contents

Ch 1 Setting the Stage for No EPA
Obama's EPA was very dangerous

When George Bush lost power, the unemployment rate was 4.6 percent and the US was doing reasonably well, other than the trumped-up market crisis of 2008. This was not doomsday. Obama made it a doomsday scenario, however, for political purposes.

Unemployment in 2016 after many double- digit Obama years, was listed as 4.7% but most of us figured that it was Obama rigging the stats again. Unless you were human, and you had to eat outside of the White House. you'd think everything was almost OK again but then again, you would be wrong. The people were so displeased that they said, No More Obama and that was also the end of Hillary Clinton.

It brought in a real tough John Wayne type guy Donald Trump, whose mission was and continues to be to save the world. Though this sounds like a promise that cannot be kept, Mr. Trump plans

on keeping his promise. What a treat having such a good man in
the spirit of Lincoln, leading our country today.

...

My objective is that this third edition book; a more blistering
indictment of a nightmare agency, will place the EPA on the
endangered species list forever. However, this species is one that
would serve mankind more by being entirely eliminated. Any
advisory or research role would be better assumed by another
agency. It would make Americans feel lots better for there to be no
EPA at all, ever again. They are out of control.

You simply won't believe how bad the EPA has become.

Check out this list of top tenners in the EPA with an extra one
added because the EPA can't even count:

The EPA's Top 11 Hits
The Clean Toilet Act
The Better Urine than Mine (pronounced my-in) Act
The Mother Nature First Act
The Single Ply Toilet Paper Act of 2018
The Don't Drive after Midnight or Noon Act.
The Chinese Light Bulb Act
The Greenhouse Gases Are Not Found in Greenhouses Act
The Sulfur Dioxide Restroom Purity Act.
The Rotten Egg Act.
The Rotten Tomato Act a.k.a. the Leachate Act of 1979
The My Globe Is Warming Act
And many others.

So much for EPA humor for now!

The EPA has become a monster in size and in its intrusive tactics.
The typical victims of the EPA are small businesses without
enough legal staff to withstand the continual onslaught. People
had been affected indirectly by the EPA through increased costs
but with the Light Bulb act, and actions threatening to make home
heating a luxury, the EPA now even terrorizes US households.

To get its dirty work done; the EPA enlists the help of other large
agencies such as the Department of Transportation (DOT), the
Department of Energy (DOE), and others. In addition to other
missions, the DOT is responsible for minimizing the exhaust gas
emissions of automobiles and other vehicles. All of this sounds
good but when the EPA is in your sock drawer for no reason, it

will be easier to tell they are up to no good. The EPA stepped in recently and gave DOT a new assignment.

DOT was forced to add greenhouse gases to its list of things that must be OK with an automobile when it is inspected. Considering the science on greenhouse gases is incomplete and far from perfect, many wonder exactly what will be measured.

As hard as it is for mere humans to believe, CO_2, some gas humans naturally and freely exhale while breathing, has been declared a noxious greenhouse gas by the human-hating EPA. Please pause to think about that. Breathing has been declared harmful to Ma Nature. Clearly the EPA has gone mad?

They do not discuss whether the exhalant must contain garlic or other malodorous scents in addition to the CO_2 for it to be declared noxious. For right now, CO_2 exhalant may be just enough for anybody's car to have a problem passing inspection with this pesky set of regulations.

…

Ch 2 The "God" of the EPA is Mother Nature

Terms such as hypocritical and a few other contemptible non-virtues at first may appear to be over-kill in describing the Environmental Protection Agency until you look just under the covers to find that the EPA is simply outrageous. The EPA is malevolent, and their decisions are shockingly corrupt, biased, and almost always anti-American. The EPA has a god. Its name is Mother Nature.

When the EPA sees man punishing their god in any way through pollution or even perceived pollution, EPA regulations are cast to punish humankind to the point of death. Ask the millions who have died or almost died in poor third world countries because the EPA believes that DDT negatively affects Mother Nature. Then ask the real scientists who have proven that DDT is safe. You will learn about this issue in detail in this book.

The EPA Is Born

The Environmental Protection Agency (EPA) was formed in
December 1970 in the US by the Nixon administration to deal
with pollution.

Nixon was certainly not an environmental whacko and there were
lots of reasons at the time to create an agency to advise the
president on matters of the environment and pollution. The stated
mission of the EPA was to "conduct environmental research,
provide assistance...[in] combating environmental pollution, and
assist the Council on Environmental Quality in developing and
recommending...new policies for environmental protection...to
the President." That's it. The EPA was not supposed to become a
guerilla anti-capitalist, pro-Mother Nature stand-alone army
engaging war against all humans and all businesses run by
humans.

A brief EPA abuse egregious example:

California farmers know how contemptible and outrageous the
EPA can be. The farmers of the highly fertile Central Valley are
being starved out of existence and denied water for growing crops
because of a small fish called the delta smelt.

The EPA offers no compromises; this bait fish used by salmon
fishermen, is winning in the courts for the EPA. California farmers
who can no longer provide irrigation for their crops and all other
Americans lost as food is in shorter supply and it is more
expensive. The progressive courts in California always take the
fish's side against the farmers. The fish lives on but the crops died,
and the farmers are on welfare. So, who really won that battle?

If it were a nasty mosquito instead of a stinky little smelt, the EPA
would still have insisted the farmers pay the price with their
livelihoods. Meanwhile American food prices are skyrocketing.
The key fact here is that farmers are human, and mosquitoes,
nasty as they are, exist in Mother Nature's domain. The EPA
loves Mother Nature and as a rule does not like humans.

The Endangered Species Act (ESA) had done positive things in the past, but in recent times it has been putting people out of work while increasing the price of food. So, if the EPA loves you and your family, why do they favor little fish over humans and why do they try to regulate CO2, which is a human exhalent? The EPA says it is a greenhouse gas and al such gasses are bad? Knowledgeable scientists, not those on the EPA payroll, see the EPA's callous disregard for humankind as impacting about every industry in the United States.

...

EPA says wear thick clothing in bed

Some say that we must rely on foreign oil because we "cannot" drill for it here in our own country. Much of our energy problems would be solved just by allowing oil drilling. Donald Trump is pro-American, and he is now getting this done.

The EPA would bristle at the thought of our country enough energy because of its impact on Mother Nature. The "cannot" part of that sentence is because there are people in the US who would be warm regardless of the EPA policies. They are OK with regular people like you and I, no longer being warm as long as Mother Nature is happy. Most of these people are part of the EPA, and the others are big rich Democrats who know their tax policies will not cost them.

The EPA abhors fossil fuels.

...

Ch 3 Barack Obama Awakened a Sleeping Nation?
Gary Hubbell Via Email

When this came into my email box, I was impressed as now I am hard pressed to explain to those not as deeply into what is happening, how the President is quickly destroying America on many fronts. This could be any chapter of any political book about this historical period. It is not specific to the EPA but it sure is a

quick look-see into what is going on while we contemplate whether the EPA is bad or good for America.
...

"Kill the EPA" was the natural title of every segment of every essay that I wrote on this topic before this was a book. My intention originally was to stop after just one essay. I naively thought that I could describe the total fallacy of the EPA in just one essay. For a writer, the topic of the "EPA" was a gift that just kept on giving as their faults are so egregious that my research turned out to be far more fruitful than I could ever have imagined.

I first verified my original thesis that the agency hurts Americans and that became the major premise. From that I concluded that such an agency does not deserve to exist, and I share the opinion of Ron Paul, in that I too believe the agency should be completely eliminated.

Humans certainly deserve to breathe clean air and eat safe food, but this EPA has too many other items on its agenda. Control of the citizenry is at the top of its list. I have concluded that the EPA cannot be trusted to do what is right for America. I am not alone in this belief.

Along the way to this book, I wrote ten original essays to explain this phenomenon known as the EPA. When placed in book form along with some other material, the work blossomed into thirteen chapters. You are reading Chapter 3 of the third edition, which clarifies items from the early edition contains new material. Thank you for selecting this book.

My objective is to spread the word and have as many Americans write their Congress as possible to get this agency out of our hair.
...
I show Gary's full email in the original book. It is amazing what the EPA gets away with. Here are the first few lines of Gary's email:

"Barack Obama is the best thing that has happened to America in the last 100 years. Truly, he is the savior of America's future. ... Despite the fact that he has some of the lowest approval ratings among recent presidents, history will see Barack Obama as the source of America's resurrection. Barack Obama has plunged the country into

levels of debt that we could not have previously imagined; his efforts to nationalize health care have been met with fierce resistance nationwide; TARP bailouts and stimulus spending have shown little positive effect on the national economy; unemployment is unacceptably high and looks to remain that way for most of a decade; legacy entitlement programs have ballooned to unsustainable levels, and there is a seething anger in the populace.

That's why Barack Obama is such a good thing for America. Here's why.

Obama is the symbol of a creeping liberalism... Literally millions of Americans have had enough. They're organizing, they're studying the Constitution and the Federalist Papers, they're reading history and case law, they're showing up at rallies and meetings, and a slew of conservative candidates are throwing their hats into the ring. Is there a revolution brewing? Yes, in the sense that there is a keen awareness that our priorities and sensibilities must be radically re-structured. Will it be a violent revolution? No!

It will be done through the interpretation of the original document that has guided us for 220 "FANTASTIC" years--- the Constitution. Just as the pendulum swung to embrace political correctness and liberalism, there will be a backlash, a complete repudiation of a hundred years of nonsense. A hundred years from now, history will perceive the year 2010 as the time when America got back on the right track. And for that, we can thank Barack Hussein Obama."

Gary Hubbell is a hunter, rancher, and former hunting and fly-fishing guide. Gary works as a Colorado ranch real estate broker. He can be reached through his website, aspenranchrealestate.com"

...

Feel free to visit

http://www.aspentimes.com/article/20100228/ASPENWEEKLY/100229854

Chapter 4 Deport All Millennials Now!

Brian W. Kelly

Deport All Millennials Now!

It ought to be easy. They'll line up like it's a free vacation

It ought to be easy. They'll line up like it's a free vacation

Book purpose:

Millennials have become a big problem that must be solved before America loses an entire generation. The parents of millennials messed up big and millennials messed up for sure and as a result they are both paying the price along with the rest of America. The purpose of this book is to show that this does not have to be a death sentence. Millennials like everybody else need redemption.

Here are a few unfortunate facts about Millennials:

1. They contributed $1.45 trillion to our national student loan debt and many of them cannot escape the burden that paying this back takes on them and the rest of society and the economy.

2. Ironically, they are as a group the most educated generation in human history, yet they have the highest share of people who are unemployed in the last 40 years.

3. 48% of employed college graduates in the millennial category have jobs that do not require a four-year degree. Thus, it seems that they are tied to a poor existence by an anvil from which they cannot escape.

4. Nearly 1/3 have postponed marriage or having a baby due partly to the recession but mostly because of their poor prospects for positive employment with their huge debts and with illegal and legal foreign nationals taking the better jobs for lower wages.

5. It is a given that millennials were raised in a world with unprecedented opportunity. When most Millennials were in middle school or high school they witnessed the birth of the Information Age. This ushered in new industries and a re-birth in education. However, their moms and dads were more interested in them receiving participation trophies that preparing them to compete in the real world.

6. Many people in other generations are fed up with the elitist notions and snobby attitudes of many millennials who appear that life owes them something, and are thus are not interested in giving them a break, plain as simple.

Millennials: can we solve this problem?

For this book, we began with a problem question that seemed appropriate. "How do you solve a problem like Maria?"

FYI Julie Andrews plays Maria in the heartwarming true story that has become a cinematic treasure. In Rodgers and Hammerstein's "The Sound of Music." Julie Andrews is Maria, the spirited, young woman who leaves the convent and becomes a... well, you know.

Who knows how to solve such a problem unless you were in the original story or in the movie or you saw the movie etc. But, at first look, I figured the problem with Maria would be easier to solve than the problem with millennials. After all, the movie seemed to solve it.

Ah! Let's just deport the millennials. But, to where? What country would take them as their reputation precedes them? It would be easier to deport Maria because we all know she is not American.

Growing up in the age of social media made this generation known as millennials obsessed with instant gratification. They need again the kind of great reinforcement that they had in T-Ball through adolescence when the participation trophies were the rage. Today, they get their kicks by being rewarded with online actions such as a "like" or "retweet."

The US workplace was not ready for millennials and maybe that's why, so many are still unemployed. Of course, it might also be that foreign nationals took their jobs. Let's not be so quick to judge.

At work, if they can find a job, needy millennials like that feely-good stuff just like the social "likes" and "retweets." They'll even settle for constructive criticism if that's all a peer can muster but they would prefer lots of reinforcement or praise, especially from a manager. This need was not in their original genes; but the need seeped in as dose after dose of feely-good stuff was always the remedy from their parents, the press, their coaches, and anybody that had to deal with them. Even good dads had a hard time denying them.

Millennials are known as the selfish generation. It is said that they need to look up the meaning of the word, friend, each time somebody accuses them of being one. They are tarred with being the lazy and entitled generation, because from my observations, they very often are. Sometimes I wonder if I am the only one who sees it?

Managers in the workplace when asked about millennials use a number of colorful words to describe them. They overwhelmingly shout out adjectives— as if recited-- "privileged, narcissistic, entitled, spoiled, job hopping Trophy Kids." This mélange is backed up with "irresponsible, and of course, unreliable.

OK, that's enough. Must we deport them? That probably would not work but it would make those who they have begun to affect lately by their rampant cynicism feel positive about something. There are a ton of ideas in this book to help us understand why millennials are who they are, and how they are what they are. There are also many ideas about how we can deal with them and how they can deal with themselves without giving up their rightful places in American History.

It is very possible that they really do have a valid beef with life. Maybe their parents and those who were supposed to give them a reality bearing failed. Maybe others are responsible for them thinking the world is all for them. I do suspect much of this is true.

Their generation is saddled with $1.45 Billion in student loan debt. They feel it because they get the dunning notices. That would keep many smiles down.

This book is written for the flawless millennials, so they can see their flaws as others see them, and know why they have them. It is written for moms and dads and kindergarten teachers and lots of others, hoping that we never put out a group of participation trophy winners like this ever again. This author believes that being a millennial is not a terminal disease and the more the patient knows about herself, the easier the cure will be.

Chapter 5 No Free Lunch--Pay Back Welfare!!!

No Free Lunch--
Pay Back Welfare!!!

A unique idea to provide a great US
safety-net and put taxpayers first

Brian W. Kelly

Provide a great big US safety-net but put taxpayers first

Book purpose:

When you loan $5.00 to a friend who is temporarily hard pressed, so they are able to buy something they need or feel they need, is it a gift or a loan? Unless it really is a gift, you always feel that one day you will be paid back. Our welfare system which includes major healthcare benefits, for some reason was never designed so that when somebody was back on their feet, they could pay back those who helped when they were hurting.

IMHO, that is the most annoying part of our welfare system. Professional welfare dwellers, even illegal foreign nationals know how to game the system for all they can get knowing nobody will ever come collecting for repayment. Even if they hit the biggest lottery or they get back on their feet and become millionaires some other way, nobody will ask them to help somebody else.

Our government somehow is too busy even to track the $30,000 or more each year in benefits they hand out per person. Something is wrong in the state of Denmark. The US needs to first account for every dime we give to anybody just like when we loan a friend a five. We should continue to help all helpless people, but we must stop making people helpless. And, when people are back on their feet, they should make some kind of payment to help a system that keeps a lot of poor people on their feet

Obamacare is welfare?

The reason there are any insured by Obamacare who actually like the program, is because the rest of the people provide it for them for free. What's not to like when things are free? The Obamacare big users get big welfare subsidies to afford their "policies," while everybody else who pays for theirs, gets poor coverage for lots of money and then they can't use their policies because the deductibles are too high. It's just the way it is. Obamacare is just another form of welfare for many people who are already getting a lot of money on welfare. In many ways, Americans are too generous. The free lunch ought to end, and soon.

When politicians refuse to repeal Obamacare to make life better for you, it is because they represent those getting the freebies, not those paying the bills. The do not care about you at all. They believe that you will vote for them anyway even though they do not represent your interests in Congress.

The big winners of course in the Obamacare lottery are trial lawyers and the big insurance companies, while the people have been left holding the bag. Healthcare has become the biggest welfare expense. In this book, we introduce the notion that all welfare, whether for healthcare or typical welfare such as food stamps and cash payments, should be paid back. We show both sides of the welfare story and offer some unique thoughts about how welfare can become an item that is paid back when people now collecting begin to do well in life.

There is no free lunch and this book shows the technology solutions that can help the US help you avoid having to pick up the tab for somebody else all their life. We enjoy describing how to account for any freeloader who takes from the system. What happens today if somebody on welfare for 50 years wins a couple hundred million on the Powerball? You bet, we solve that problem too. It's in here.

Table of Contents

Preface

How about a free lunch? The US government gives millions of lunches away every day in one way or another. Did you get one today?

When I updated this original 2008 book about then current, domestic, political and constitutional issues intertwining with public consciousness, I became immersed, once again, in that vortex of all-too-familiar concerns about our government. I was compelled to add a few paragraphs about the Obama presidency considering the transparent failures of the coronated administration.

As I undertook the task of updating, I became so smothered in the existential issues that had since developed that I was pushed to delve further into the examination of the underlying issues. Thus, the project moved beyond what one may consider to be a standard update/ revision to the point that, when I received the book back from the editor, I noticed that she had split the original book not once but twice and had created two additional, entirely distinct books.

An update to the first book, Obama's Seven Deadly Sins, was released concurrently with the predecessor of this book in summer 2016. It advises that the deadliest sin of all is indeed Obama's approach to healthcare, or what many now call Obamacare. This book's predecessor, Healthcare and Welfare Accountability was already within Obama's Seven Deadly Sins as a chapter and when split, it was first released as Healthcare Accountability.

In summer 2016, in the middle of the Trump presidential campaign, I modified it to reflect how a future Trump presidency might view such accountability. Here I am again with President Trump at the helm of the Big Ship US. Now we examine what President Trump should consider doing in the area of accountability. I make some very strong recommendations.

The Editor noted that the book offered a coherent, common sense solution to the biggest problem with US healthcare for all -- its huge cost. It happens that much of the same overall solution can be applied to the current high-cost US welfare system, the theme of this book.

She suggested that it be released as its own separate offering and that's what I originally did but now we are at round three. The original book, Healthcare Accountability offers a unique and compelling solution to the problem of healthcare cost. It is still available on Amazon & Kindle.

This book title, *No Free Lunch – Pay Back Welfare* hits the nail on the head as a way to provide a safety net while not being played as a fool or a chump.

Those following the healthcare debate note that President Bush and President Obama both agreed that a database of health records needed to be established on behalf of the people. It is a good idea. There needs to be a record of each citizen in the United States so that it will be much easier to get a full picture of a patient in any medical provider setting from doctor's offices, laboratories, imaging, and other specialties.

Can you believe that there is no such database for welfare? In other words, for all the dollars the US spends on welfare, there is no database in the sky that a president, or his staff, for example can query that can give a report on, say, the number of children, whose parents collect welfare. Government officials must guess.

Most Americans are aware of the major battle on health insurance and healthcare "reform" as in Obamacare, which after eight years, continues to brew in the Halls of Congress even today. A Democratic Congress and the former POTUS decided by themselves to spend a trillion dollars on a government take-over of healthcare in 2010. They stole about $700 million from Medicare, weakening that program, and still many seniors think Obama was the finest of all presidents.

They knew it would possibly improve the lives of just 17% of the people and seven years later even that number has not been achieved. With 325 million in our population, just 10 million in total are signed up for Obamacare. Despite it being illegal, many foreign interlopers receive Obamacare benefits due to fake IDs. Obamacare is so insignificant as a real healthcare solution; however, it should be on nobody's agenda. Its significance is that it destroyed the healthcare opportunities for the rest of the country.

When the bill passed, Congress willfully disrupted the lives of the other 90% of Americans by providing them with less healthcare, less medical provider choices, huge deductibles, and more taxes. You cannot take $700 billion from Medicare for Obamacare and make Medicare better. It is an insane thought. Perhaps senior citizens will have to find employment again to buy back what was stolen by government without their permission?

Obamacare's big users get big subsidies to afford it or nobody would be enrolled. Healthcare is the biggest welfare expense. In this book, we introduce the notion that all welfare should be paid back when the recipients have become more productive citizens.

There is no free lunch and this book shows the technology solutions that can help you avoid having to pick up the tab. Milton Friedman, the late great US economist coined the term, "There is no such thing as a free lunch." Somebody always pays. The rest of us pay for Obamacare welfare.

In this accountability book, we describe, in reasonable detail and in words that any American can understand how to make the healthcare system -- both ER and Medicaid, and the remnants of Obamacare more accountable to the people.

Since we believe as a nation that there is no free lunch we must gain accountability in welfare and healthcare. We must begin to keep track of things. May I repeat that President Bush and President Obama both agreed that a database of citizen health records needed to be compiled and it is, indeed, a very good idea.

When President Trump slogs through all of his early to-dos, we can bet that he too will agree that a database of electronic health records for citizens is a great idea and we need to make it work. I suspect he will also be impressed with a Personal Accountability System that keeps track of everything Americans have given to other Americans from the time this system began.

In such a system, there would be health records and payback-accountability records for each citizen in the United States. In this way, it would be much easier to get a full picture of a patient in any medical provider's setting. It would also help us all know who owes what back to Uncle Sam and the people. You go in, give your cards, and poof, the provider you have never met has your permanent medical record known as an Electronic Health Record.

This book provides a logical and clear blueprint that defines the terms for organization of online database records and discusses the entities that are positioned to "own" your health data. It also offers suggestions specifying which entity would be the proper custodian of such vital data. Hint—not government or insurance companies.

This book on accountability identifies the best means of managing the collection of health records in a "system in the sky." Additionally, the book helps Americans understand the issue and gives a solution that assures privacy and locks out the bad guys who want your health data so badly they can taste it. As a bonus, it offers a cogent solution for welfare accountability.

Why did Brian W. Kelly write this book?

Brian W. Kelly wrote this book because he cares, and as the publisher, I am publishing this book because I care. This book points out many of the issues and makes a case for patient accountability and then shows how it can be achieved. It identifies the best means of managing the collection of health records in a "system in the sky."

Additionally, it will help you understand the issue and give you a solution that assures your privacy and locks out the bad guys who want your health data so bad they can taste it. As a bonus, it offers a cogent solution for welfare accountability. President Trump would do well to have his team evaluate this book for adoption into the overall Master Builder's Plan.

I hope you enjoy this book and I hope that it inspires you to take action to help the government of the United States to stand firm against any attacks on democracy from without or from within.

Stopping politicians from giving away the resources of the country to buy votes is a good way to start. When President Trump drains the SWAMP, we intrinsically know things will be better. A little accountability can go a long way.

I wish you all the best
Brian P. Kelly, Publisher

Ch 1 Should Welfare Be Paid Back?
A never-ending question if at a bar!

Can you imagine being at a bar and you are the somebody who shouts out: "Don't you think welfare benefits should be paid back? You might not get positive credit for the discussion but by the end of the session, morning or evening, you would get enough different answers to make you question your original thinking on the subject. It is a hot potato.

Should welfare be paid back? Among other places, to find that people think about it, I went to the http://www.topix.com/forum, and the first comment was the kind of idea that if brought out in public, would definitely generate a lot of talk. Forums are in many ways places where John and Jane Does can talk anonymously as if they had a few schnorkies in front of them when talking, and who cares? Check out this forum post by a guy who wants to be known as Why Not. Mr. Why Not gets our discussion rolling with some definite opinions:

Just hit myself in the head with an idea.

On another thread I was trying to explain why a loan was different from a gift as it applies to food stamps and welfare.

Then it hit me. Why don't we make people pay back benefits such as food stamps and welfare? Computers are wonderful (at times) because they can remember anything that is entered into them.

Let's keep track of all benefits people receive in the way of food stamps and welfare, including SSI. If they ever receive a tax refund, lottery winnings, etc. let's take the benefit money back first. Say these people eventually make it big, earn twice the poverty level, etc. make them pay it back. Kinda like child support.

What do you think?

I was fishing for ideas before I wrote my third version of this book, which takes another hard look at welfare accountability. My wife calls it research. So, we are all on the same page, Merriam Webster defines accountability below and then they give the perfect example a group that is rarely accountable:

Accountability is the quality or state of being accountable; especially: an obligation or willingness to accept responsibility or to account for one's actions. Example -- public officials lack accountability.

In my research, I learned that there are a lot of thoughts on paying back welfare by people who would not give up a penny as well as those who would be willing to give away the whole store. Most have good reasons for their feelings on the issue based on their own experiences in life.

For example, here is a direct response to Why Not that is completely the opposite in the feelings it generates:

Some food stamp recipients are old, elderly and sick living on a fixed income. They may have worked hard all their life, and are really not happy they are on assistance, but it's get the assistance or be homeless and hungry. How are they going to pay it back? Especially if they die and have no estate?

Should the food stamp recipients be pushed off the cliff in a wheel chair?

Let's take a shot at an answer for that question. If I ran the US Welfare, Inc. and the numbers showed that the situation for which the old, sick, food-stamp recipients, living on a fixed income had not improved, then the only correspondence sent to the recipient would be a summary of benefits sent once a year along with a Merry Christmas note. To do this, of course, the US would have to collect such information. The men in the black coats with the big cars would not come collecting to somebody in dire straits.

Paying a debt back when you are able is not freeloading. Unless an individual is physically able to work, and there are job opportunities, and the choose not to take them, their benefits even in a payback system as I propose should not be affected at all.

Ch 2 Welfare Debate Among Americans
Do Americans care: You bet we do!

There are two sides to every issue. In a debate about welfare conducted online recently the participants were asked whether welfare in the US should be ended. That may be an easy question to ask but it is a tough question to answer.

Many of the debate participants highlighted the abuses of which they know first-hand and also through the tales of others. Knowing that the abuses actually are paid by them through their taxes is naturally upsetting to normal Joes and Josephine's.

Nonetheless, there are those who look only at the good intentions of welfare, and they choose not to see the abuses in the implementation or the greed of the abusers. Such good people do exist though if the world were run according to their precepts, I fear everybody would be motivated to choose to be helpless.

Consequently, there are many opposed to suggesting welfare be shut down completely. This first comment starts out asking us all to check our souls before we answer the question:

"What would Jesus say/do?"

The comments in this debate are put forth with quotation marks and they are indented. My opinions and observations of their comments are shown directly after without quotes and without indentations. I hope this engenders some good thinking among the readers.

> "I know it's a cliché to say what would Jesus do. That being said, what would He do? Most Americans call themselves

religious and the majority of those would put the check mark on the Christian box. So, with that, why would the same people simple call welfare *lazy people who drain us and basically are a waste of air?* I don't get it. Jesus always spoke about how the weak will be saved and all that stuff. Most Americans would say that they are Christians, but I guess it's easier to say we are something than actually be something."

"Bad things happen to good people, and if the people standing do not help the people that fall down then we are doomed. It's as simple as that. I wonder how many of the people who voted yes have actually been successful in life with absolutely no help from anyone whatsoever. The truth is EVERYONE in life has been helped by someone else, and unfortunately some people have to go to government."

My favorite retort to those who wish we simply increase welfare amounts and forget about what it does to those just getting by who pay the taxes, is coming. It also applies to those who have been able to position themselves as welfare recipients. This comment gives away my feelings on how we should conduct our welfare business in the US.

"I am 100% behind helping helpless people but I am not as much as 1% in favor of making people helpless." Remember the title of this book is not *No Lunch!* The Title of this book is *No Free Lunch!* Why would anybody that has been fed during hard times object to paying something back to benefactors when times for them are better? Answer me that, Riddler?

The following opinion piece strengthens my argument even further:

The poor are better off without welfare. Ask Kansas Gov. Sam Brownback. Opinion piece by Christian Schneider, Opinion columnist Published 7:53 a.m. ET Aug. 11, 2017 | Updated 9:56 a.m. ET Aug. 11, 2017...
https://www.usatoday.com/story/opinion/2017/08/11/cutting-welfare-helps-people-christian-schneider-column/557082001/

Sam Brownback: It is not the good intentions of government programs that matter, it is the bad incentives.

(Photo: Charlie Riedel, AP)

"In J.D. Vance's hit 2016 autobiography <u>Hillbilly Elegy</u>, he tells the vivid story of rural Midwestern whites trapped in a cycle of poverty and unemployment. Preeminent among the colorful characters who populated Vance's life as a young man was his grandmother, "Meemaw," a strong, salty old woman who did not possess a filter between her thoughts and words."

"Meemaw believed much of the poverty in her Middletown, Ohio neighborhood was caused by government handouts that incentivized the poor to not work. Among the invectives she lobbed at her neighbors: 'She's a lazy whore, but she wouldn't be if she was forced to get a job'; 'I hate those f_____ (the government) for giving these people the money to move into our neighborhood; I can't understand why people who've worked all their lives scrape by while these deadbeats buy liquor and cell phone coverage with our tax money.' "

"While intemperate in her observations, new data show that, at least relating to her larger point, Meemaw might have been on to something."

"A study by the conservative-leaning Foundation for Government Accountability tracked more than 6,000 Kansas families 17,000 individuals who were moved off of cash assistance in 2011 when Governor Sam Brownback instituted new work requirements for welfare recipients".

"The data show that families who left government assistance under the new work requirements saw their incomes double within one year of leaving welfare. Within four years, their incomes nearly tripled, as they earned nearly $48 million more in wages than when they received a government check."

Of course, without programs such as those instituted by Governor Brownback, the couch would have remained the home for the eternal couch potatoes in Kansas for perhaps all of eternity. Taxpayers would be paying for their largesse without much impact on the real problem. Moreover, nobody would have known that they could do much better including the potatoes themselves.

WC Fields often said, "Never give a sucker an even break, and never smarten up a chump." Americans today feel like suckers and chumps as the community organizers and others supporting Welfare, Inc, have an army of lawyers at the ready to bilk normal Americans out of their hard-earned income at the drop of a hat.

Think about that and ask if it is asking too much for the government to keep track of the bills it pays for whom.

Ch 3 Americans Do Not Always Agree
Grocery cashiers know more than you would believe.

Nobody sees how welfare recipient's rip-off the system more than the cashier at the local grocery store. Some cashiers are very ungracious after work as they report their experiences at the local gin mill. Here is one such story:

"As if it wasn't bad enough knowing that The Government was giving my hard-earned money to young, totally capable, but unwilling, and lazy, high school drop-outs, I as a cashier get to personally hand out the food that those food stamps and WIC checks paid for to the young and lazy "Useless Trash of America" (as i refer to them)"

"And I have to do so, to support myself but as a (let's call it a side-effect) I am simply Making more money to be taxed and given to the Trash. It is a horrible cycle, that I am simply SICK TO DEATH of."

"And as if this didn't grind my gears enough, I work at a very High-end (High-priced) grocery establishment, therefore not only are they buying food with my money they are buying expensive over-priced food. And not essential food like milk eggs and bread, Pop tarts and $5 bags of high-end chips, and Sushi (Pricey anywhere) and then pull out their own cash (I'm sure they didn't really earn or at least wasn't taxed). In order to pay for their cases and kegs of alcohol and bulk packs of tobacco."

"Now I make no joke when I say I could quite literally go on typing ALL NIGHT, but I will end it here by saying there has existed a single principle since the very beginning of the human species or life itself for that matter that I STRONGLY believe we should follow today. And that saying is, as we put it in the South where I live: "YA DONT WORK, YA DONT EAT!"

…

We all know that the problem is that the government aka Congress wants Americans to be indebted to them for any improvement in their lives. Instead, Americans should fire these representatives to even the score. Nobody in America should go cold nor should they be hungry. However, when things are good, those saved by the system in my opinion should insist on helping to pay back those who are now hurting.

Chapter 6 Wipe Out All Student Loan Debt—Now!

Unique solutions to the $1.45 Trillion debt accumulation

Book purpose:

There are lots better solutions to the problem of seventeen and eighteen-year-olds having been persuaded to dig a huge hole in their lives with no escape so that they can attend college. Somehow, the same banks or financial aid offices would not loan a 17-year-old enough to buy a bike, or a car and certainly not a house. Yet they are willing to loan a house-worth of cash, so a kid can go to college.

They don't promise a job after four years when they take that $100,000 from the kid. They don't even promise a degree. Worse than that, they don't promise anything close in value to its $100,000 price tag. No wonder 1 out of 6 borrowers default when the time comes to pay back the loan. And, the rate of defaults is getting even worse.

More than half of the 45 million former student borrowers are struggling to pay back $1.45 trillion. The big winners in the rigged student loan game are the universities and the loan sharks. Instead of student-loan bankruptcy being against the law it ought to be against the law to give so much money to a kid who cannot make a living after graduation. We all know that sociology majors, no matter whether they get a prized $20,000 per year job or not are going to be struggling all their lives in such a crowded field. Yes, it ought to be against the law.

The more I researched this topic the more I felt that students have been fraudulently abused by big Universities, big loan sharks, and the big Obama era student loan officials. Elizabeth Warren on Saturday, September 26th, 2015 in a speech about Obama's takeover of student loans blasted his administration for being piggy by charging usury-level interest rates.

It seems that student loans from the federal government issued between 2007 and 2012 are on target "to produce $66 billion in profits for the United States government." So, not only is the government ripping off student borrowers on the loans, they are making a big profit, the purpose of which of course is to help fund Obamacare.

I once thought this problem could be solved by a combination of lower interest rates, some forgiveness, etc. I no longer think a piecemeal plan is the correct solution. Why did I change my perspective?

I fear that an entire generation of students, mostly millennials, will be lost and will never be found again unless drastic action is taken now. And so, I call for legislation that wipes out all student debt now. Wait until you see what such an act does to boost our economy beyond expectations. In this book, I offer some great ways in which we can pay for the write-off without hurting taxpayers.

President Trump knows a ripoff & a rigged system

President Trump in understandable terms has netted out the student debt crisis from both a student and parent perspective: "They go, and they work, and they take loans, and they're borrowed up, and they can't breathe, and they get through college and the worst thing is, they go through that whole process and they don't have any job." Trump has it right, and worse than that, when the US system hurts them, our best and brightest lose hope.

Many have excoriated the Obama Administration and government and coffee-breath professors who teach nothing, for making it worse for college graduates. They all make money on the student loan program. Trump says: "You know the one program that the U.S. makes a whole lot of money with is student loans, and that's maybe the one program they shouldn't be making money with... "So, we're going to have to start a program," he said. "We're going to do something very big with loans because you have to get these people going. They really feel down and out."

Donald J. Trump is right. Yet he is the only president who has even talked about solving America's problem with rip-off loan sharks and a government that makes big money off the backs of student borrowers. Ironically, the man willing to help is hated by the very young Americans he speaks about helping.

College graduates and those former students not fortunate enough to complete their degrees need all the help they can get to claw their way out of their college debt. Your author as a professor and as a father understands student debt. He feels and has intellectually analyzed the plight and the pain felt by today's millennials. Besides recommending a total forgiveness and a do-again, this book also examines other ways to solve the problem including refinancing, extending, and providing better payment plans as well as getting universities to put some skin in the game.

This book addresses the massive $1.45 Trillion student debt already on the books and it presents a boldly unique plan to assure that students with loans have a chance of success with a job of their choice. Isn't it about time? This book tells you how it can be done. You won't be able to put this book down before you know what you can do to help those with student debt be able to afford homes and start families and live the life of a real American and not an indentured servant.

Preface:

Rarely does a book title explain exactly what a book is about. This book is the exception. Wiping out all student loan debt now will immediately solve the student debt crisis. There is no question about it.

It will also kick start the economy with such a punch that Americans will be talking about how great it is that America is so great again. Additionally, it will bring back a whole generation of lost souls with no chance in life—the millennials—so they can lead normal lives like all other generations before them.

It helps to recall that President Obama increased the National Debt by $9.1 Trillion in just eight years, hoping to assure that illegal aliens had all the resources they needed to take as many American jobs as they could. He just about doubled our debt and has nothing to show. Tell me where the money went? It was spent but what good did it do?

What if we had taken a small piece of that expenditure and paid off all student debt? Wow! What if at the same time so it never happens again, we put in measures to assure that 17-year olds could never be sucked into giving up the promise of a real life for a fake-news promise of prosperity ever, ever again.

It is too bad that he did not have the foresight to use $1.3 Trillion of that wasteful largesse to help America. With less than 15% of this reckless, aimless crony capitalist spending, the former president could have been a folk hero among many Americans.

He could have and should have spent more wisely and wiped out 100% of the student debt now strangling our young American adults and holding the US economy hostage. Until the student debt crisis is put behind us, the most physically capable and more than likely, the brightest people in America, our recent college graduates between the ages of twenty and forty, will not be part of the American game of life.

They will not be in a position to start a business, buy a home, new appliances, a new car, or begin a family. I am talking about 45 million student loan borrowers—seventy percent of all college students / graduates. At a time that we needed Obama's leadership the most, right after the sub-prime mortgage crisis when the economy was at a standstill, how could the former president have missed the opportunity to reinvigorate the economy by freeing 45 million young people from debtor's prison.

The former president had the opportunity to reinsert forty-five million Americans with a propensity to spend money into the economy and he did not choose to act. He chose not to free them from the shackles of repaying a massive and unfair student debt load that will keep them out of the economy for years and years to come.

This book tells Congress and the new president how to solve the crisis and it tells Americans that nothing happens without a vigilant population. That means we must hold our government and our politicians accountable for solving this crisis that affects almost every family in America.

More and more Americans, even those of us who have paid off all of our student debt are looking at today's student loan dilemma much differently. The groundswell of concern for removing so many potentially productive Americans from the economy at one time is at an all-time high with more Americans asking Washington to forgive this debt so that young Americans can engage and so that the economy can be jump-started to make all Americans successful.

Young Americans are literally choking on their student debt. It has their lives stopped and each year that it not solved is another day in a veritable debtor's prison. It is so bad that 50% in a recent survey would be willing to give up their most fundamental freedom to be able to lead a normal life.

A survey from Credible, conducted through Pollfish, hits the seriousness of the situation right on the head. It is understandable that young Americans would want a chance in life by having their debt removed. But it was surprising to many what they would be willing to do to be free of those loans. The most popular answer the 500 respondents between the ages of 18 and 34 chose for what they would be desperate enough to sacrifice was "suffrage." Yes, half surveyed said they would give up the ability to vote in the next two presidential elections to be able to move their lives forward.

It is not just those who would be set free who feel forgiving student debt is an idea whose time has come. More Americans believe that the US should forgive all federal student debt than feel that the recipients should pay their loans back. The results to many of the survey conducted by MoneyTips.com were shocking. Nearly 42% agreed with the statement, "I believe President Trump's Department of Education should forgive all federal student debt to help the economy."

Those who paid off their student debts on time with no issue have a right to be upset by the thought of others getting such a huge break. I paid off my own student debt without help from anybody else. But the amount was nothing like the life-ending loans that today's millennials face. So, many default, and they basically end their lives despite in many cases having a college degree.

So, I asked myself if it helped me in anyway if somebody else got a break in life. Let's say they may have been sucked in at 17 years of age by an admissions counsellor with a big quota who never would have loaned the kid $300 of their own money for a junk car. Yet, they had no problem taking taxpayer funded loans and giving these kids $100,000 and a promise of a great life—a life that never happened for far too many. How would it hurt me if they were helped?

Less than 37% disagreed, while the remaining 21% neither agreed nor disagreed. Some of those who disagreed are hard-core about it as they struggled and paid their loans back but again, why keep somebody poor who made just one bad choice in life.

Even those who for years were pressuring Congress to do the right thing were taken back by the overwhelming response to help these former kids become adults. For example, Brandon Yahn, founder of "studentloanguy.com said: "It is surprising that the majority of the US population supports this measure...Perhaps this student debt burden has spread more across all generations, and popular sentiment is turning the corner as it relates to student debt."

What country would wipe out opportunity for almost a full generation of its citizens when the Congress itself is partially responsible for the easy money these kids spent on an education that brought them no benefits.

When asked further about the positive impact on the economy and the impact of future student's ability to attend college in the future, most believe that this is a one and done. There should never be another forgiveness. And, so the consensus is that there needs to be a fool-proof solution for new student debt so that new high school aspirants to college do not sign up for debt when they do not need to do so.

There are a number of notions in this book besides wiping out all of the (now) $1.45 Trillion. This book discusses most if not all of the theories about how this happened and how it can be made to never happen again. Additionally, it discusses a number of student resources and a few tricks that are both honest and long overdue.

Why did Brian W. Kelly write this book?

Brian W. Kelly wrote this book because he cares about college graduates being able to move on with their lives. I am publishing this book because I care. This book identifies the most notable and most serious flaws in student tuition financing. It then solves them by prescribing a number of Kelly-unique solutions to help get the program back on track.

I hope you enjoy this book and I that it inspires you to take the individual actions necessary to help the government of the US stand firm against any attacks on democracy from outside or from within this great country. A great start of course is to stop the government gouging of young Americans, who are plagued with student debt. Instead government should be a helpful tool in solving this deep moral dilemma for our country.

I wish you the best.
Brian P. Kelly, Publisher
Wilkes-Barre, Pennsylvania

Table of Contents:

Ch 1 The Best Student Debt Solution
Congress must have the will to act

There are many solutions for student loan debt at different levels discussed in this book. The first and the best solution is depicted in the title of the book: Wipe Out All Student Loan Debt Now! It is clearly the ideal solution from an American point of view and it has economic ramifications that along with the new tax plan can add to a major jump re-starting of the economy. The ideal solution would be to wipe out all of the student debt from all college loans. There are many ways the US can afford this and prosper because of it.

This act alone would free forty-five million debt-ridden former college students, mostly graduates to go ahead and get real lives for themselves. They will be in a position to start a business, buy a home, a new car, and begin a family.

The negative impact of so many student borrowers is clear. Essentially, the US has 45 million Americans, who are putting a big chunk of their monthly income towards their student debts. That means that they aren't spending on other economy-boosting goods or services. This group also has less money to save, invest, or even start a business. The burden is so heavy that over 8 million (and growing) have stopped paying a dime. This phenomenon is called being in default.

Three other Opinions on canceling Student Loan Debt

I am not the only person who thinks it is a good idea to start over again on student loans and wipe what we have off the books as soon as possible. Here are three other opinions as to why it is not only a good idea; it is a great idea and the US can not only afford it; the country will profit from it.

David Muccigrosso, an Armchair Economist, blogging at //www.quora.com, on Feb 12, 2013 took a shot at answering this important question: What would be the economic impact of forgiving all US student loan debt?

At the time this was written in 2013, student loans and debt in the US exceeded credit card debt, at just over $1 trillion. Now the debt is closer to $1.45 trillion because there have been no major changes made by colleges and universities to assure new student debtors will be able to pay back their loans. Here is David's piece:

"Around 80% of that is guaranteed by the federal government, with the rest belonging to private lenders.

"Theoretically, winding down all student loan debt would proceed like a national, publicly organized bankruptcy. The federal government would start by forcing lenders to take a "haircut" (significant discount to outstanding principle) on the loans it's guaranteed, and it would allow private loans to be consolidated as federal loans for the purpose of being put through this program as well.

"Winding down $1 trillion in debt is hard in any circumstance. This will be even harder given the sheer amount of bitching the financial sector already does about the federal government. The program would probably take from $500 to $800 billion in total spending (equating to a 50-20% haircut for investors) - roughly the same magnitude as the Bush stimulus package.

"Most banks would not be crippled, but the financial sector would still have a hard time dealing with the hit to their balance sheets...

"The other major problem would be that a program of this magnitude would destroy the student lending market as we know it. Higher education finance would have to be replaced by a spending package on the order of at least $1 trillion and involving some higher taxes to provide free universal public higher education - the only real option once you've taken debt-financed education off the table. (TBH, I'm actually in favor of a less dramatic version of this whole wind-down and conversion, but this incarnation is just too unworkable)

"On the plus side, those suffering under student loan burdens would have a lot of income freed up. You'd probably see surges in multifamily unit construction (apt buildings), the auto industry, and nightlife/entertainment spending, but the economic activity wouldn't cancel out the huge Wall Street "shit fit" that would be simultaneously occurring.

Forgive student loan debt to stimulate the economy.

Originally Written – January 29, 2009
By – Robert Applebaum at http://studentdebtcrisis.org

Back in 2009, President Obama signed into law a $787 billion stimulus package on top of Bush's grossly mismanaged $700 billion TARP bailout from September. That is more than the total student debt of today, $1.45 trillion.

Shortly thereafter in 2009, the Federal Reserve basically printed an additional $1,000,000,000,000 to inject more funds into the monetary system, which will undoubtedly have the effect of diminishing the purchasing power of the dollar. Now, we are approaching twice the total of all the student debt. In other words, if we acted then to forgive the debt, it would be all gone, and all paid for.

Since then, the US government has paid out trillions of dollars in bailouts, handouts, loans and giveaways, with no end in sight as our leaders tried to do anything and everything to get our spiraling economy under control. While some of what Washington has already done may act to stimulate the economy, much of the trillions of dollars already spent will, no doubt, has proven to be just money wasted.

Tax rebate checks **do not** stimulate the economy – history shows that people either spend such rebates on paying off credit card debt, or they simply save them, doing little to nothing to stimulate the economy. Presumably, that is why they were removed from the final version of the stimulus bill.

The tax cuts that were included, however, amount to a whopping $44 per month for the rest of 2009, decreasing to an even more staggering $33 per month in 2010. This is hardly "relief" as it is likely to help nobody.

The Wall Street financial institutions, auto manufacturers, insurance companies and countless other irresponsible actors received TRILLIONS of taxpayer dollars (as demonstrated above, that's a number with *12* zeros at the end of it) to bail them out of their self-created mess. This, too, did nothing to stimulate the economy. It merely rewarded bad behavior and did nothing to encourage institutional change.

There is a better way

How many times have we heard from our leaders in Washington that education is the key to solving all of our underlying societal problems? The so-called "Silver Bullet." For decades, presidents, senators and members of Congress have touted themselves as champions of education, yet they've done nothing to actually encourage the pursuit of one on an individual level.

Some of us have taken advantage of Federal Stafford Loans and other programs, including private loans, to finance higher education, presumably with the understanding that an advanced degree equates with higher earning power in the future. Many of us go into public service after attaining such degrees, something that's also repeatedly proclaimed as something society should encourage.

Yet, the debt we've accrued to obtain such degrees have crippled our ability to reap the benefits of our educations, causing many to make the unfortunate choice of leaving public service so as to earn enough money to pay off that debt.

Our economy is still in the tank, though with Trump already we are seeing great signs of relief. There isn't a reasonable economist alive who doesn't believe that the economy has needed a real stimulus for a real long time.

The only debate now centers on how to go about doing it. While the new stimulus plan contains some worthy provisions, very little of it will have a significant and immediate stimulating effect on the economy. The Obama Administration itself in 2009, did not expect to see an upsurge in the economy until mid-to-late 2010.

Instead of funneling billions, if not trillions of additional dollars to banks, financial institutions, insurance companies and other institutions of greed that are responsible for the current economic crisis, why is not a better idea to allow educated, hardworking, middle-class Americans to get something in return? After all, they're our tax dollars too!

Forgiving student loan debt would have an immediate stimulating effect on the economy. With Trump, we are already back to 3.3% GDP growth. Who knows what having 45 million ready to spend, millennials reengaged in the economy will do for the country?

Responsible people who did nothing other than pursue a higher education would have hundreds, if not thousands of extra dollars per month to spend, fueling the economy now.

Those extra dollars being pumped into the economy would have a multiplying effect, unlike many of the provisions of the 2009 era stimulus packages. As a result, tax revenues would go up, the credit markets would unfreeze, and many jobs will be created. Consumer spending accounts for over two thirds of the entire U.S. economy and in 2009, consumer spending has declined at alarming, unprecedented rates. Therefore, it stands to reason that the fastest way to revive our ailing economy is to do something drastic to get consumers to spend.

This proposal would quickly revitalize the housing market, the ailing automobile industry, travel and tourism, durable goods and countless other sectors of the economy because the very people who sustain those sectors will automatically have hundreds or, in some cases, thousands of extra dollars per month to spend.

The driving factor in today's economy is fear. Unless and until the middle class feels comfortable enough that they'll have their jobs, health insurance and extra money to spend not only next month, but the month after that, etc., the economy will not, indeed, cannot grow fast enough to stop the hemorrhaging.

Let me be clear. This is not about a free ride. This is about a new approach to economic stimulus, nothing more. To those who would argue that this proposal would cause the banking system to collapse or make student loans unavailable to future borrowers, please allow me to respond. I am in no way suggesting that the lending institutions who carry such debts on their balance sheets get legislatively shafted by having them wiped from their books.

The banks and other financial institutions have already gotten their money regardless because, in addition to the $700 TARP bailout, even more bailout money came their way. This proposal merely suggests that in return for the Trillions of dollars that has been and will continue to be handed over to the banks, educated, hardworking Americans who are saddled with student loan debt should get some relief as well, rather than sending those institutions another enormous blank check.

Because the banks are being handed trillions of dollars anyway, there would be no danger of making funds unavailable to future borrowers.

To avoid the moral hazard that this plan could potentially create, going forward, the way higher education in this country is financed MUST be reformed. Requiring students to amass enormous debt just to receive an education is an untenable approach, as demonstrated by the ever-growing student loan default rates.

Having a loan-based system rather than one based on grants and scholarships or, ideally, public funding, has, over time, begun to have the unintended consequence of discouraging people from seeking higher education at all. That is no way for America to reclaim the mantle of the land of opportunity.

A well-educated workforce benefits society as a whole, not just the students who receive a higher education. It is often said that an undergraduate degree today is the equivalent of a high school diploma 30 or 40 years ago. Accepting the premise as true that society does, in fact, place the same value on an undergraduate degree today as it did on a HS diploma 30 or 40 years ago, then what is the rationale for cutting off public funding of education after the 12th grade?

It seems to me that there is some dissonance in our values that needs to be reconciled. That, however, cannot come to pass until the millions of us already shackled with student loan debt are freed from the enormous economic burdens we're presently carrying.

Many of the vocal nay-sayers to this proposal seem intent on ignoring the fact that Washington will continue to spend trillions of dollars, likely in the form of handing blank checks over to more and more banks, as a way of getting the economy under control. Normative assessments of how things should be, are fine, but they don't reflect reality.

Accepting the premise that Washington will spend Trillions of dollars in unprecedented ways (a good portion of which will just be trial and error, since we're in uncharted waters), what is the argument against directly helping middle class people who are struggling, rather than focusing solely on the banks and other financial institutions responsible for the crisis to begin with?

Further accepting that there is an aggregate amount of outstanding student loan debt totaling approximately $550 Billion, (that's Billion with a B, not a T), [even more in 2017] one is forced to ask again, what is the objection to helping real people with real hardships when all we're talking about is a relative drop in the bucket as compared with what will be spent to dig us out of this hole?

In a perfect world, I share these biases towards personal responsibility and having people pay back what they owe and making good on the commitments they've made. But we don't live in a perfect world and the global economy, not just the U.S. economy, is in a downward spiral, the likes of which nobody truly knows how to fix.

This proposal will immediately free up money for hardworking, educated Americans, giving them more money in their pockets every month, addressing the very real psychological aspects of the recession as much as the financial ones. Is it the only answer? No, of course not. But could it help millions of hardworking people who struggle every month to get by? Absolutely.   Support real change we can believe in!

More Americans Want to Forgive Trillion-Dollar Student Loan Debt Than Want It Repaid

MoneyTips http://www.ajc.com
4:00 p.m. Friday, July 21, 2017 Business and Money news

More Americans believe that we should forgive all federal student debt than feel that the recipients should pay their loans back. In a shocking survey recently conducted by MoneyTips.com, nearly 42% agreed with the statement, I believe President Trump's Department of Education should forgive all federal student debt to help the economy. Less than 37% disagreed, while the remaining 21% neither agreed nor disagreed.

"It is surprising that the majority of the US population supports this measure," says Brandon Yahn, Founder of studentloansguy.com. "Perhaps this student debt burden has spread more across all generations, and popular sentiment is turning the corner as it relates to student debt."
...
While income wasn't a factor, gender seemed to affect people's feelings on this subject, with more women favoring forgiveness over men. 47% of the women agreed or strongly agreed with the statement, while less than 36% of the men felt the same way.
...
Reasoned millennial money expert Stefanie O'Connell, "Women are now more likely than men to get a college degree, which may explain why they would favor student loan forgiveness at higher rates. They're also likely to experience career interruptions due to childbearing and caretaking, which can impede their lifetime earning potential and, consequently, their ability to pay back their loans.

Finally, many of the lucrative jobs that don't require a college degree tend to be in male-dominated fields - carpentry, electrical, etc. - which might explain why more women favor loan forgiveness."
...
Says Student Loan Hero, expert Miranda Marquit, "Many millennials, who thought they were doing the right thing, took on student loan debt only to graduate to an economy where jobs have been scarce, and wages have been mostly stagnant for decades. Gone are the days when you could work for the summer and pay for the following school year.

As a society, we sold a dream and failed to deliver. You can make payments on your loans for decades and barely make headway." Adds Marquit:

"As a result, these millennials are unable to help the economy in other ways. Research indicates they are putting off financial milestones that come with economy-building benefits.

"All the consumption that comes with things like buying homes and starting families is being lost because the largest generation yet doesn't have money to spare. Student loan forgiveness would go a long way toward helping millennials feel stable enough to take the next steps in their financial lives, as well as even starting businesses."

Ch 2 No Problem Is Without a Solution
The government is not your friend

Despite self-serving governmental, political, and academic apologists suggesting that there is no real student debt crisis, just ask a recent millennial graduate when they hope to start a family. You better have a lot of time. We keep hearing about a student debt crisis. Yet, politicians continue to argue that there is no student debt crisis though everybody else knows that there is. Perhaps the definition of a crisis can tell us--a time of intense difficulty, trouble, or danger.

The fact is that recent students with major loans are having trouble paying them back. The fact is that they have put off major life plans until their personal crisis improves to manageable.

Is the country in crisis? Whether the country is in crisis or not, taxpayers are now on the hook for about $1.45 trillion outstanding in student debt. That makes student debt substantially larger even than credit card debt. Moreover, it's not looking like it's going to get any better in the future. The graduating class of 2017 owed an average of over $37,000, up from less than $30,000 in 2014.

...

In its #issues 2012 of American Voices, in a piece by Maureen Tkacik of Reuters titled: The student loan crisis that can't be gotten rid of, from August 15, 2012. In this snippet, piece, you get to see three situations where there was a clear abuse of power by the thug student loan collection industry.

"A military veteran sharing his story with Occupy Student Debt has paid $18,000 on a $2,500 loan, and Sallie Mae claims he still owes $5,000; the husband of a social worker bankrupt and bedridden after a botched surgery tells Student Loan Justice of a $13,000 college loan balance from the 1980s that ballooned to $70,000. A grandmother subsisting on Social Security has her payments garnished to pay off a $20,000 loan balance resulting from a $3,500 loan she took out 10 years ago, before she underwent brain surgery." How is this fair? Is this what Congress actually wants?

Ms. Tkacik strengthens her case for some compassion by Congress below:

"You have probably mentally cataloged the student loan crisis alongside all the other looming trillion-dollar crises busy imperiling civilization but also enrich the already rich."

"But it is different from those crises in a few significant ways, starting with the fact that the entire loan business is arguably unconstitutional. You don't have to take it from me: A pre-eminent bankruptcy scholar made precisely this argument under oath before Congress."

"In December 1975, when Congress was debating the first law that made student loans non-dischargeable in bankruptcy, University of Connecticut law professor Philip Shuchman testified that students: 'should not be singled out for special and discriminatory treatment. I have the further very literal feeling that this is almost a denial of their right to equal protection of the laws ... Nor do I think has any evidence been presented that these people, these young people just beginning their years on the whole should be singled out for special and as I view it discriminatory treatment. I suggest to you that this may at least in spirit be a denial of their right to equal protection with the virtual pole star of our constitutional ambit.' "

Ch 3 Is Student Loan Game Rigged?
Do Colleges & Universities have unfair advantages?

You bet they do!

It costs Academic Institutions nothing when students come out
sacked with a lifetime of debt after four to six years with no jobs.
Donald Trump can recognize a rigged game better than any man
in America. He can sniff them out and call them out and /or play
against them and still win. He thinks the student loan game is
rigged against students and it favors the universities and the
government disguised as loan sharks.

Trump does not like that the game is rigged, and he has promised
to fix it. The President believes that Universities must have some
skin in the game for any long-term solutions to be built.

Many people are affected by the crisis and, so it is a topic at the
dinner table in many homes—especially in those homes in which
the student loan invoices are beginning to arrive from junior's or
missy's four or five year past sojourn into campus life.

When people in the US discuss the student debt crisis, most focus
on how it affects them personally. If they are not directly affected,
they discuss the rapid growth in outstanding debt and its impact
on the economy and the country.

They may also discuss some of the recent milestones, which are
not very positive. For example, student loan debt exceeded credit
card debt in 2010 and it exceeded auto loan debt in 2011. It is
rapidly rising, and it passed the $1 trillion mark in 2012. It is
currently at about $1.45 trillion and growing.

It is a big problem. The Wall Street Journal recently reported that
More than 40% of student loan borrowers are either in default,
delinquency or have postponed repaying their student loans. It is
a crisis and having the federal government making over $45 billion
off the backs of student borrowers in excessive interest payments
does nothing to help matters.

With about 40% of students defaulting on their loan paybacks—
mostly because the payments are so large, is a problem for all

America. It is also a big disgrace for a country that does not want to be labeled as "Third World."

These milestones don't tell us much about the impact of all that debt on the students themselves. Seventeen and Eighteen-year-olds are making lifetime decisions even today with little counselling other than "Don't Worry! Be Happy!"

These naïve high school seniors were originally told by a friendly College Financial Aid Officer that everybody borrows, and it is a privilege to be able to attend this college with the help of the university's loan package.

Does that sound familiar. If Joe's Hot Car Lot was scamming young adults at the same rate as academia, the Justice Department would shut them down. At least Joe's Hot Cars can make it around the block. What about the kids with $50,000 in debt, no degree, and no job?

Sometimes as learned by default interviews, there was never an up-front discussion of the loan impact when it came time to repay it. As hard as it is to believe, the loans came so easy that 53% of the students when graduating, did not even know there was a payback. And we all know what payback is!
...

70% of all college students have borrowed and many who are already enrolled still have more to borrow before they finish their degrees and then have to pay for their college education. It is a national travesty.
...

Can you imagine the major spark in the economy if all of a sudden, millennials became the big spenders and were enabled to throw house parties in homes they never thought they would own?

The fact that Obama's government made about $43 Billion a year in many years, by charging higher than reasonable interest rates on student loans shows that solving the debt problem was never a priority during the last eight years. Let's hope Mr. Trump looks past Obama to create a system that works.

Chapter 7 Boost Social Security Now!

Brian W. Kelly

Boost Social
Security Now!

Hey Buddy, Can You Spare a Dime?

Hey Buddy, Can You Spare a Dime?

Book purpose:

The mainstream economists and the media tend to ignore the truth regarding the consumer price index. The CPI is really not indicative of the actual inflation rate as the Bureau of Labor Statistics (BLS) purports. With too much skin in the game, this government tool has engaged in methodological shenanigans over the past couple decades that are directed at depriving seniors their true cost of living annual increment. This is well documented by John Williams of ShadowStats, among others.

All their monkeying with reality means that the official rate of inflation is listed as two to five times lower than the actual rate. This is very convenient if you are a government bureaucrat trying to hold down interest costs and Social Security payments. It is not such a nice thing for seniors trying to avoid their next home being the poorhouse.

It is not surprising that "deep thinking" coffee-breath professors are on the side of liberals in government rather than the people, including their own grandmothers. Americans depend on the truth for an honest cost of living adjustment—something which has not happened in over thirty years. In other words, the government has been flat out lying to reduce its obligation to seniors.

From my own analysis of the shadowstats.com work, seniors should be receiving amounts that are over 4X their current checks. This is a travesty and must be corrected as more and more seniors are becoming destitute, having to make choices like paying property taxes or buying bread and milk. My recommendation is to right this wrong and not by a generous 2% margin as has been the best in five years. We must immediately boost the COLA rate for 2018 to 15% and to report expenses fairly, we must put Medicare increments into the calculation.

It is puzzling how Medicare can go up by exactly the same amount as the SSR COLA and yet not count in the COLA? The fake CPI put out by the BLS is simply a fraud, and the chained CPI planned for the future is an even greater fraud. The CPI must be corrected, and back pay is well due seniors. If the government fixed the game and began to give 15% a year beginning this year for at least four years, I think most seniors would forgive public officials for their thirty years of chicanery.

Why would a country punish senior citizens?

The most beleaguered citizens in the United States are our senior citizens. Seniors are victims of government. It should not be so; but it is easy to explain. There is not one senior citizen member of Congress, who actually depends on Social Security to make ends meet. How is it then that they get to cast their magic wands annually to determine the cost of living increase due seniors. They feel none of the pain of seniors—none!

Congressional inflation estimates unfortunately are nothing close to the reality of the real price increases seniors actually pay every-day at supermarkets and clothing stores in America? The law on SSR has been distorted and seniors need and deserve a massive adjustment. It is up to seniors to make sure Congress knows that it has not delivered. Perhaps when seniors are the reason for members being sent home for good after the next election, the Congress will understand.

If President Obama had another heart, some say it would be lonesome. For eight years, seniors served as the former President's personal punching bag as he stubbornly refused to give seniors a break. Obama even tried to reduce senior benefits with his chained CPI proposal. Then, he took more than $700 Billion from Medicare to fund his signature legislation known as Obamacare.

Democrats, the ones who claim Republicans have no hearts are all Tin Men on the SSR issue and their main man for eight years, Barack H. Obama had no regard at all for Seniors. He claimed otherwise but worked to reduce SSR benefits for the duration of his eight years in office. He simply could not sneak it in without hurting the Democratic Party, so they stopped him.

Wimpy Republicans without the courage of Donald Trump, permitted the former President to decrease the livelihood of seniors and chose not to fire back at the former president with the gumption they now show when opposing Trump. They chose to do nothing to help seniors.

Mike Huckabee was the first Republican to complain when he publicly accused "illegals, prostitutes, pimps, (and) drug dealers" of freeloading off the Social Security system during the first GOP primary debate way back on August. 6, 2015. This freeloading must be paid back to seniors. Despite President Trump's problems with Republican RINOs, seniors pray he still has the energy to help.

During his campaign, candidate Trump promised to protect Social Security without cutting benefits. I wrote this book to help remind the new President that a huge SSR monthly increase is the right medicine and it must be done ASAP before more seniors suffer.

Seniors, if denied the proper increase, need more than just accepting the bad medicine of the past. They need to be paid back for the abuses to the system over the years that Mike Huckabee and others have cited. If you don't have a mom or a dad who are hurting because their Social Security "check" does not even pay for their meals, you can't know how bad it is in America for "poor" seniors.

What should President Trump do in the absence of any Congressional leadership? His positive actions would include paying back Medicare from Obamacare. It would include increasing SSR benefits over the next four years of the Trump term by at least 15% per year.

Even this will not make up for what was stolen from seniors using a fraudulent cost of living percentage. President Trump knows that revenue flows from elimination of waste, fraud, & abuse and he can direct that American oil reserves can provide ample cash for strategic emergency make-up funding for senior benefits.

What would you pay to see every senior in America smile because buying a fresh loaf of bread and a dozen eggs is no longer a big issue in their lives? Seniors ask for nothing more than to be made whole for the intentional fraud in Congress's CPI calculations and to use an accurate measurement of the cost of living and the out-of-pocket expenses endured by seniors.

My concern is that the good President Trump, as the sitting president, may be so insulated from the reality he knew as a candidate, might sit idle and permit an unfair inflation rate put more and more seniors in the poorhouse.

The President must make up for all the past bad CPIs at once. American can take care of her seniors if we so desire. In this book, we tell you how things can and must be made lots better for penniless seniors, whose scant increases get wiped out all the time by Medicare increases. You'll be surprised as to how much sense the proposal to Boost Social Security now makes. It is the new senior credo and mantra. President Trump cannot let seniors down.

Table of Contents

Preface:

Congress & the President must act now to avoid a bigger crisis!

Somebody will say that the US cannot afford to pay for seniors to be OK! I say that we cannot afford not to do what is right. This is America.

If somebody says we cannot afford to assure that seniors can lead lives in which the poorhouse is not a constant threat, please tell them to read Chapter 11 of Boost Social Security Now from start to finish and use their imagination. America and Americans can do anything we choose to do. We in the Boomer generation learned that growing-up. Unfortunately, that message of truth has been diluted recently by Democrats trying to do nice things for illegal aliens at the expense of seniors.

We can afford making seniors whole again and we must. The dirtiest politicians in America colluded so they would not have to take the real cost of living into consideration for the last thirty years or so. Nobody in America wants this perpetration to stand, especially seniors who just lost their homes and who are now scraping to find a good meal.

My dad, as I grew up in the 1960's told me often that Roosevelt's Social Security was not welfare. He loved Roosevelt's programs to save those who might not be well-off in the future of America as they aged. Everybody had to contribute to SSR, so that all Americans could retire with dignity. The Congress of the USA, shame on them, have brought a period of indignity upon seniors through fraud, and they should be held accountable.

For eight years of President Obama's regime, it was not very safe to be a senior citizen. It is still not safe. President Trump has a mission to learn how poorly seniors in the middle class and lower have been treated by the US government. Many seniors are hopeful things will change.

In former president Obama's heart, he had to know that this batch of seniors did not trust him very much to do the right thing by them. Seniors got exactly what they expected from Obama – nothing. Five zero or almost zero cost of living raises were the order of the day in eight years while Obama seemed to be smiling about the savings he had secured off the backs of seniors.

Only low information seniors, and there are far too many for the good of the US senior citizen population, continued to the end to give the former president the benefit of the doubt. I guess this was because they listened to the corrupt mainstream media and read the biased New York Times.

They may have received lots less than ever before, but they loved President Obama nonetheless. He had the gift of gab and for many, he was a fine pied piper. They would follow him anywhere and they still will even if they die of starvation. My advice for other seniors is start reading to these guys the facts of our nation every day.

The reality is that even today, starving seniors do not fault the former president, though they would if they really knew what he did to them. Worse than that, if they knew how bad he tried to make it, but failed, seniors would be enraged. You'll learn what that was in this book. President Obama did his best to destroy the lives of senior citizens. He knew seniors did not trust them and he was a great guy for a big payback for his detractors.

As noted previously, it is a documented fact that the most beleaguered citizens in the United States today are senior citizens. Why is that and why should it not change immediately with a kinder Trump administration? Some seniors are so respectful of authority that they become dumb when a Democrat suggests they have it made because of all great Democratic programs—even when their cereal bowl is empty in the morning. Unaffordable raisins and other fruit in the cereal bowl should not be on the menu. How about we all try living on that.

For eight years, any senior paying attention, and not part of the love-fest, noticed that they were serving as former President Obama's personal punching bags. He knew that in their hearts, many, who knew what he was up to had little regard for him.

They had him pegged right as a man who would take away their last drop of water if he could—if they promised to die quietly.

They were right. There is lots more inside this book to help seniors move to action to assure that SSR increases are fair and that the government brings seniors back to where they should be—after all the government lying on the inflation rate.

Yes, I am talking about large annual increases in COLA for the next eight years to help seniors get back most of what they lost because of all the fraud associated with the government's cost of living adjustments.

You are going to love this book as it tells it like it is. Feel free to contact your Congressman and President Trump so that they know how you feel. One day we will all be seniors.

I wish you all the best
Brian P. Kelly, Publisher
P.O Box 621 Wilkes-Barre, Pennsylvania 18703

Ch 1 Hey Buddy, Can you Spare a Dime?
2018 SSR Benefits raise for seniors is net of "0"

There is no official abbreviation for social security or social security retirement. Therefore, in this book we will use our own abbreviation SSR to mean social security as well as for social security retirement. As many know, the German Army in World War II commandeered the term SS and, so we will stay away from any negative connotation by staying away from that abbreviation.

When President Trump was inaugurated, the paltry increase from President Obama's last year in office was .3%. That is .003 for those like me who want to really know where the decimal point is.

I don't think that President Trump intended to slam seniors like Obama did; but they got slammed nonetheless as Obama's last approved increment was implemented by the newly elected President Trump. Seniors who think this President does no wrong are now hoping he sees what happened throughout the Obama years and about thirty years before, and that he adjusts things retroactively to where they should be.

My sources say that the COLA received v the COLA which should have been applied to senior retirement income is in the neighborhood of 4X. That means that SSR recipients would be getting $2000 per month instead of $500.

It may be hard to believe because most Americans would never think that their precious Congressmen, who they live intrinsically would ever permit that to happen. When I ran for Congress in 2010, the 26-year, 13-term Congressman I hoped to replace had already stiffed his senior constituency of about 2.5X of the 4x. That means if they were getting $500, they should have been getting at least $1250. As my dad would say once it is gone. "Try and get it!"

The potential benefits increase for millions of seniors in 2017 was expected to be larger than usual to make up for the past abuses by government in calculating the inflation rate. After Obama's almost-zero last rate at .3%, President Trump's announced rate at 2% for 2018 is admittedly about six times more than the $5 buck raise per month in Obama's swan-song. But, it shows no deference to seniors who feel things the Trump family has never felt.

The paltry increase still does not make up for the actual inflation rate's impact on seniors' income. Moreover, it does nothing to counteract the intentional lowball CPI official inflation rates, endured for over thirty years. These cost seniors many thousands of dollars, even though they were fraudulent. Seniors who do not pay attention to the screwage, need to figure out how to ask for what Roosevelt promised them. Send your Congressman home if he does not reply.

In government the left hand takes what the right hand gives. Seniors in 2017 already got the bad news that Medicare premiums for physicians' services rose again and would rise again in 2018 and again. Thus, Medicare, buy the design of a Congress that gives less than a damn for seniors, will consume the entire cost-of-living adjustment for most seniors for 2018 again.

It is hard to believe that the same government that thinks seniors should get 2% to help with increased costs and out of pocket expenses, is stealing back the 2% for Medicare. Why are such costs not included in the COLA? No government costs which are clearly known are mitigated. Seniors lose again. But why? Hey Buddy, Can You Spare a Dime?

Brother, Can You Spare a Dime? is a 1975 documentary film starring Walt Disney, Bing Crosby, Charlie Chaplin, Andrews Sisters, Fred Astaire, Shirley Temple, Eleanor Roosevelt, and Franklin Delano Roosevelt. It was produced by Image Entertainment, consisting largely of newsreel footage and contemporary film clips to portray the era of the Great Depression and the tough times experience equally by most Americans.

To the rest of the Country, the Trump era is now bringing in prosperity that has been absent for at least eight years. But, not everybody is gaining. Seniors are still suffering through the Great

CPI Depression, with its major inflation tax. So far, there is no recovery in sight.

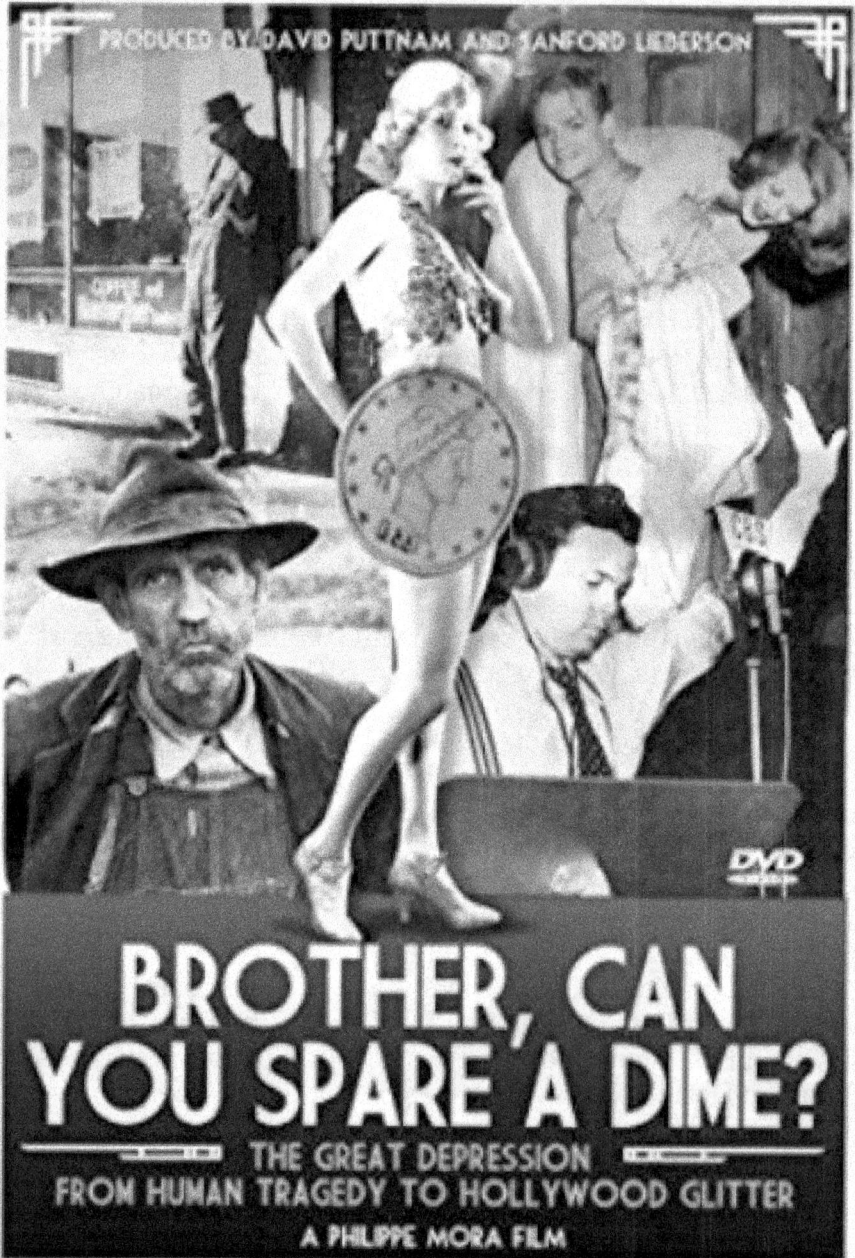

PRODUCED BY DAVID PUTTNAM AND SANFORD LIEBERSON

DVD

BROTHER, CAN YOU SPARE A DIME?

THE GREAT DEPRESSION FROM HUMAN TRAGEDY TO HOLLYWOOD GLITTER

A PHILIPPE MORA FILM

"Brother, Can You Spare A Dime?"

They used to tell me I was building a dream
And so I followed the mob
When there was earth to plow or guns to bear
I was always there, right on the job

They used to tell me I was building a dream
With peace and glory ahead
Why should I be standing in line
Just waiting for bread?

Once I built a railroad, I made it run
Made it race against time
Once I built a railroad, now it's done
Brother, can you spare a dime?

Once I built a tower up to the sun
Brick and rivet and lime
Once I built a tower, now it's done
Brother, can you spare a dime?

Once in khaki suits, gee, we looked swell
Full of that Yankee Doodly Dum
Half a million boots went slogging through Hell
And I was the kid with the drum

Say, don't you remember? They called me 'Al'
It was 'Al' all the time
Why don't you remember? I'm your pal
Say buddy, can you spare a dime?

Once in khaki suits, ah, gee, we looked swell
Full of that Yankee Doodly Dum
Half a million boots went slogging through Hell
And I was the kid with the drum

Oh, say, don't you remember? They called me 'Al'
It was 'Al' all the time
Say, don't you remember? I'm your pal
Buddy, can you spare a dime?

Will Donald Trump come through for seniors?

It gives me no pleasure to say that Donald Trump will get little more than one more year of good will from seniors. In too many ways, today's times for seniors remind me of the peasants rotting in the Russian gulags. Looking for any hope, they found every excuse to forgive Joseph Stalin for their plight. "If only Joseph knew!" They believed 100% that somehow if he only knew, Stalin would do something to help them.

Chapter 8 Legalizing Illegal Aliens via Resident Visas

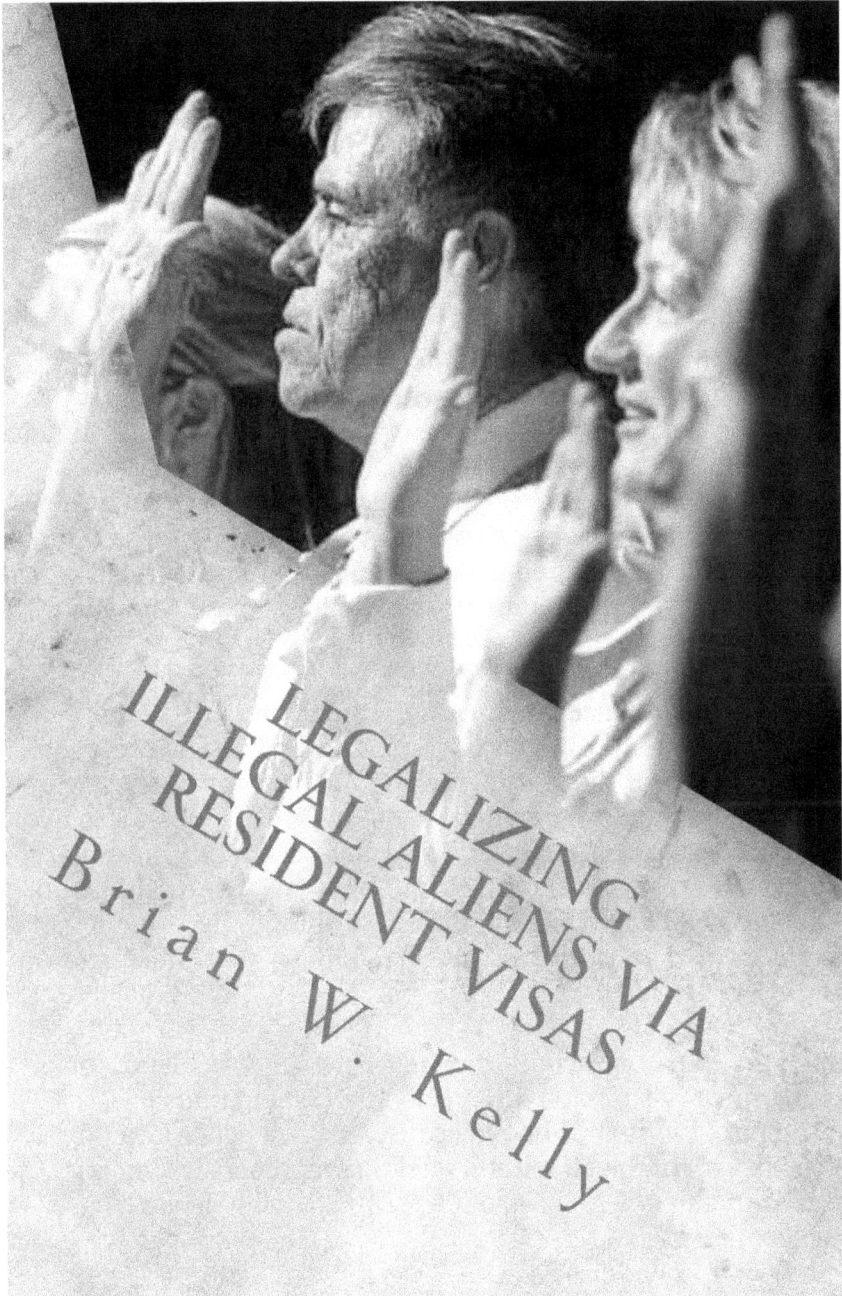

LEGALIZING ILLEGAL ALIENS VIA RESIDENT VISAS

Brian W. Kelly

A great Americans-first plan which saves $Trillions. Learn how!

Book purpose:

Despite our best efforts pre-Obama, after the 1986 Reagan Amnesty, the flow of interlopers across the border and from visa overstayers brought in from 1 million to 4 million illegal aliens per year. Obama's lax immigration policies in which he basically told our Border Patrols to stand down made matters even worse over the last eight years.

Meanwhile, many Americans forgot they once had jobs and they began to believe that their depressed wages caused by illegal immigration would never abate. Maybe it was their fault. Former president Obama took no action in eight years to protect Americans and so when President Trump ran for President, there were many who had been affected negatively and they voted for Trump en-masse. They hoped that the flow of illegal foreign nationals would stop and that we could deport those who had entered illegally.

Liberals try to convince Americans that there are just 11 million illegal foreign interlopers, but nobody is buying it. The same song has been played for the last ten years. John McCain's estimate is 128 million and my own estimate is 60 million. These people live in the shadows, take American jobs, and for each one on welfare, they cost US taxpayers about $30,000 per year. The total is about $500,000,000,000 per year and the effect of low wages and no jobs on Americans is another $500,000,000,000 per year. It has to stop now.

Despite the toll on our country, most Americans see deporting 60 million or even 11 million foreigners as cruel and unusual punishment. I wrote this book because I have a better idea. We can legalize all of the 60 million after a comprehensive vetting process and a first-year fee of $200.00 and $100.00 in each subsequent year.

If the interlopers agree to the provisos and are approved after vetting, the one-time interlopers would receive an annually renewable new type of visa, called a resident visa.

To gain and keep their resident visa status the interlopers would promise to take no welfare and no free healthcare and no freebies of any kind. If they don't take our offer, and they do not take the Pay-to-Go offer, they will be deported.

They must have their own or employer provided healthcare. They can keep their current jobs, but all Americans would be considered first in line for any new jobs. Additionally, they must promise never to vote in any American election and unless they go back to their home countries, they can never get in line for citizenship.

No Sanctuary Cities or DACA needed

There would no longer be a need for sanctuary cities, and the DACA problem would be solved for each of the "DACA people" who are approved for the resident visa. There is lots more. The major benefit for illegals is that they are out of the shadows and the major benefit for Americans is that they are first for jobs and the country saves about $500 billion in welfare costs each year.

The notion of a resident visa permits us to solve the problem of 60 million interlopers without any deportations other than for criminals and unsavory characters. It is a permanent program that puts Americans first in all matters. It is such a good idea that it can actually replace the green card and the notion of anchor babies. Instead of birthright citizenship, anchor babies would get a resident visa with no welfare.

What today are green card holders, would get a special resident visa as a citizen designator if they otherwise would have qualified for a green card. If they are not citizens within the ten-year designation, they would lose the citizen aspirant designation. No illegal foreign national legalized under this program would be eligible for a citizen aspirant designation.

What if a current interloper does not want to give up welfare benefits. Such a person can sign up for a companion program covered in a book titled, Pay-to-Go. A stipend of from $20,000 to $50,000 plus transportation costs will be paid to anybody in former illegal status or in green card status or anchor baby status. They can take a nice bundle of cash to their home country with each family member receiving a substantial amount. Their families can be reunited in their home countries with enough proceeds to become successful entrepreneurs.

Democrats still want the interloper vote

Everybody knows that the objective of the left during the Obama presidency was to get as many illegal foreign nationals into the country as possible. Into the country for when the big amnesty comes, Republicans won't be able to get elected as dog-catcher.

The Atlantic argues that this is a new position of the Democrats who once were for regular Americans, but now are for every group on the fringe and are no longer nationalistic in perspective. Here is what they say in a piece written in 2017:

"In 2005, a left-leaning blogger wrote, "Illegal immigration wreaks havoc economically, socially, and culturally; makes a mockery of the rule of law; and is disgraceful just on basic fairness grounds alone." In 2006, a liberal columnist wrote that "immigration reduces the wages of domestic workers who compete with immigrants" and that "the fiscal burden of low-wage immigrants is also pretty clear." His conclusion: "We'll need to reduce the inflow of low-skill immigrants."

"That same year, a Democratic senator wrote, "When I see Mexican flags waved at pro-immigration demonstrations, I sometimes feel a flush of patriotic resentment. When I'm forced to use a translator to communicate with the guy fixing my car, I feel a certain frustration."

The blogger was Glenn Greenwald. The columnist was Paul Krugman. The senator was Barack Obama. See how much they have changed. Today, even these three champions of the left would have their Democrat cards pulled for uttering such speak.

Americans have not changed. We are still not at all happy about any amnesty. Thus, no solution for the 60 million interlopers living freely in the shadows of America with no fear under former president Obama-style protections can come without Americans being the winners.

The Resident Visa Program as proposed in this book takes a hard look at Americans who do not want to deport illegals en-masse, yet want the country back under full American control. Foreign Nationals should have no say and certainly no vote. Looking at the reality of our times, it is time to offer Americans a solution to the 60 million residents that we can live with and with which, all Americans can prosper.

The fact is that nobody in America but a few of the unsavory variety, want the stain of deportation on their own souls. We can solve the problem in a pro-American way without requiring coerced deportations for non-criminals. Let's get criminals out as quickly as possible.

Even liberals ten years ago recognized that the border-hopping low-skilled immigrants depressed the wages of low-skilled entry level American workers and strained America's welfare state. No kidding! But, something happened between then and now. In 2008, the Democratic Party platform called undocumented immigrants "our neighbors, but it still offered some cautions. By 2016, the immigration section of the platform didn't use the word illegal, or any variation of it, at all. The former illegals had become future voters. This really upsets Americans who pay more than lip-service to America. Why the change?

The brutal truth is that illegal aliens vote, and in large numbers. Voter fraud is not exclusive to illegal aliens, however. There are also legal aliens (green card, H1B visas, tourist visa holders, etc.) who vote illegally. Democrats are pleased to look the other way.

What do Americans want? Check out the list of the top five items that Americans want before they would agree to any form of legalization.

1. Only Americans vote
2. No welfare for non-citizens. That means no free cash, medical services, education, or welfare services / benefits.

3. Employers must hire American citizens first
4. No amnesty or citizenship
5. Must speak English

The Resident Visa Program (RVP) as proposed in this book provides these assurances for Americans. For an illegal foreign national to be granted such a visa, they would be required to swear that they agree 100% with the five items Americans care most about as well as others that would be part of a total resident visa package.

One at a time, candidates for the RVP would pay $200 each to be vetted. If accepted, they would gain a one-year residence pass known as a resident visa, paperwork, and an ID card that must be kept on their person at all times. Their visa would be renewable every year for $100.00 as long as they remain model residents, a term which will be defined to mean all aspects of "keeping their noses clean." This visa is intended to take all illegal foreign nationals out of the shadows and into the light of day. There may also be some fines and fees for having broken American law that can be paid "on account."

The cost savings for Americans are immense.

No analyst estimate on the cost of illegal aliens is below $100 billion per year. When all of the services are totaled up, there are estimates of cost savings higher than $500 billion. America can save $500 billion or more per year by enacting this legislation.

Additionally, there are studies that demonstrate the costs that are born by Americans per year for illegal foreign nationals lowering wages and taking the jobs of Americans. This is estimated at another $500 billion per year.

It would not take even five years for most of these dollars to begin to flow in America's favor. This is a big economic deal for Americans.

Among other things, this automatically solves the DACA problem and the sanctuary city problem. No sanctuaries are necessary when everybody can be legal and productive in the US

Additionally, different forms of the Resident Visa can be created so that we can do away with all of the benefits such as welfare that come with green cards. There would be substantial cost savings there. Rather than ten-year renewable permanent residents in line for citizenship, those who would be green card holders under today's program would become Resident Visa holders instead and those in the green card program would change to resident visa holder at their ten-year renewal. This special visa form would permit citizenship.

No former illegal alien who becomes a resident visa holder under this program would ever be able to change status to get in line for citizenship. Only by going back to the home country and approaching it legally from there would this be possible.

I wrote another book titled Pay-to-Go, which is examined in this Top Ten book. Pay to go demonstrates the major cost savings that would accrue to the US by providing huge stipends as high as $30,000 for illegals who agree to permanently depart the US for their home country.

America is not the only country in this bind of having too many residents from foreign countries. Countries as far away as Australia have problems with migrants taking native jobs. They use a technique called the Assisted Voluntary Return as part of an overall Pay-to-Go plan to incent migrants to leave Australia and return back home. They are OK with these migrants going home with or without Aussie assistance. As noted, one of the books you will take a peek at in this book is titled, "Pay-to-Go." That book explains it all.

This notion, which is not an American idea, across the globe, pays both travel expenses and offers a generous stipend for those in potential despair who sign up for the offer to return home. Then, they arrive home with a lot of bucks in their individual pockets. They get to start businesses, and take care of their families and for them, the American dream helped to deposit them in their home country with a wad of cash that they could not have gained by themselves in a million years, which they are entitled to use in order to prosper in their home countries with their families. Should life be so good?

But, then in America, there are those who do not wish to leave. What about these? They have no interest to leave the USA no matter what the incentive may be? Should they be left behind when the boat pulls out for their home countries? Maybe so! Maybe not! But this is America not their homeland and we must always be for Americans first.

Are we Americans better off with the remainder of 60 million illegal interlopers staying in the shadows of America, rather than devising a plan to solve the problem in a way that keeps America whole and makes Americans the masters of our own country again?

The last official try by eight corrupt US Senators to right this wrong was called the Gang-of-Eight plan and it basically gave up America and Americans for the benefit of the illegal interlopers. It put them on a fast track to citizenship that would cost US taxpayers up to $6.3 Trillion with all of its provisions. In 2013, Americans told Congress nyet, and the House voted "no" and we sent the Gang of Eight Senators packing but they still are hanging around.

Unfortunately, if we do nothing to end the tremendous cost and sacrifice of accommodating the 60 million illegal interlopers in the shadows of the USA, we cannot sustain our resolve to be free again of oppressive congressional actions.

Will this scurrilous gang of 8 re-emerge and take Americans down? How long can we Americans withstand this situation, which many rightfully call A Mexican Standoff. Our country is clearly in chaos. We see a race to the bottom in wages that is underway; and regular Americans suffer by losing the jobs and low-wages war every day.

Meanwhile, there is no American consensus as Democrat-dominated American cities and certain Democrat states have decided to offer sanctuary to illegal foreigners rather than to American patriots. They choose not to support the needs of American citizens. The point is that if we Americans opt to do nothing, this real standoff in the USA is scheduled never to end. Democrats have chosen to stand against regular Americans who love America.

The one clear choice for those wishing to stay in America would be if we can legalize interlopers with no benefits at all. This would end the sanctuaries and the shadows and be good for everybody. I think we can do it. That is what this book is about.

In this book, you can read about how to legalize Illegal Aliens via a new notion called a resident visa. It takes interlopers out of the shadows and gives them the opportunity they seek while keeping Americans whole and keeping the country prospering with Americans in charge. You're going to like this America-first plan built by an American for Americans,

Brian W. Kelly

Preface:

What would you call a plan that solved a problem for America that most of the Congress seem to have no interest in solving? I have called it many things while perfecting this book, but now let me settle my mental rumblings with what it should be called The Resident Visa Plan. It has a companion plan called the Pay-to-Go Plan, another book that is highlighted later in this book.

Legalizing Illegal Aliens Via Resident Visas is the first book of two recently introduced. Together, both books fully address the solution to 60 million interlopers residing in America. The second book, that has been released is the companion book. Its title is Pay-To-Go.

Both of these books should be required reading for every House and Senate member as well as the President of the United States. Together, these are the only plans that can work for Americans-first—to end the shadows and the sanctuaries and save America about a $Trillion per year. Both books are available on the Amazon and Barnes & Noble sites.

The Resident Visa Plan is a vision for a secret sauce solution to fix the problem of 60 million interlopers waking up in America every day without our permission. Yes—build the wall, please! But simultaneously solve the residence problem of so many people who do not belong here in America.

What American believes that we really need up to 60 million interlopers in residence? I do not think so. Hey, John McCain thinks there are over 128 million interlopers in residence. Maybe he is right. Do we need 128 Million? Can anybody tell me what we need? My personal thoughts say we need zero illegals. It is time to give Americans an opportunity to work in America.

I am very pleased that you are reading this book and I hope many others find it and convince the US Administration and the Congress and the President that it is their turn to learn about The Resident Visa Plan. It should have been obvious without me, a guy from no place giving the Congress and the President such a good idea, but I am very pleased to do so.

The Resident Visa solution is unique, and everything needed to implement it is already in place. It directly addresses the issues that having 60 million illegal foreign nationals in residence have brought upon America. Nobody likes deportation but just like you would throw an uninvited guest out of your house, it would be very fair for the US to throw out (deport) the 60 million uninvited guests in America today.

Yes, deportation is fair of course as these folks have broken our laws. But, our politicians are culpable as they made it too easy for foreigners to break our laws. The problem is that we do not see them in our house every day and so most of us have no stomach for deporting them.

Therefore, an adjunct solution to the Resident Visa Plan is a Pay-to-Go Plan. The US will pay the return expenses for each illegal interloper who chooses to return to their home country. Moreover, depending on their status in the USA, the government will provide a generous stipend of anywhere from $20,000 to $50,000 once they return. That's a good deal.

Amnesty is not a solution as Americans have already paid a big price for the largesse of politicians wanting low wages and those wanting the future votes of today's interlopers.

Ideally, the solution would be to go poof, and every foreign interloper would be taken back to where and when they crossed the border years and years ago.

Every plan requires fine tuning and we would expect this to continue to be the case with the Resident Visa Plan. When illegal interlopers do not want to be paid to go, and they want to stay in the US, the Resident Visa Plan comes in very handy. Together these plans are the long-sought solution to 60 million illegals in America. Nobody will be illegal and there will be no need for sanctuary citizens.

Instead of birthright citizens, those born in the US with resident visa parents would automatically become resident visa holders with the yearly fee waived until they hit 21-years of age.

A key element of this plan is that each year the clock resets on foreign nationals who are permitted here on a temporary basis under the Resident Visa Plan. This book, thus focuses on interlopers signing up to become Resident Visa Holders with appropriate renewal assurances for good behavior.

In summary, this book presents the Resident Visa Plan as the fix and the Pay-to-Go Plan as the backup fix. Then it offers many other points on why this is the one and only fix to create an America without shadows that favors Americans 100%. There is so much good left over that good-willed interlopers have a lot to gain simply by signing up.

You are going to love this book as well as the plans themselves. All interlopers immediately are to be registered and accountable. You will see that The Resident Visa Plan is designed by an American for Americans idea whose time has come.

Additionally, illegal foreign nationals will be very pleased because the plan uses deportation as a very last resort and it immediately gets illegal foreign nationals out of the shadows. Few books are a must-read, but this highlighted book and The Resident Visa Plan will quickly appear at the top of America's most read list.

This is a simple, America-first solution but only if Congress and the President have the guts! It solves the problem with 60 million interlopers in America and many others!

Table of Contents

Ch 1 Is There a Solution?
60 million interlopers cost taxpayer dollars

If we knew how to immediately stop the drain on our government treasury with one bold and very fair move, would America's inept politicians make that move? I have done many analyses and I have concluded that American politicians, from Congress and the Senate on down. will never support Americans unless convinced that they would be out of office otherwise.

Based on what it costs to support illegal foreign nationals (average of $30,000 per person per year), the US can certainly afford to deport millions of people. But, the dirty politicians and the corrupt press preach a different mantra that puts Americans last and illegal aliens first.

Ironically, though Americans complain about all of the illegal aliens, supporting them, having them take their jobs, and lowering the average wages in America, most would prefer a different solution than rounding them up and deporting 60 million people.

But, we can afford deportation if we choose. If nobody was collecting welfare, this would be a lot tougher, and if nobody in illegal status was stealing from Americans, maybe no American would care.

Can we afford a mass deportation of illegal foreign nationals—even without a roundup?

Is there a consensus for or against the idea? It only matters if the US can actually afford to undertake a mass deportation?

Let me prove that we can afford deportation before we move on to solutions that we can stomach. I am not recommending mass deportation, but we can certainly afford it and the US can save lots of money if we chose to do it.

Let's say that 30 million of the 60 million illegal aliens in residence collect some form of welfare from the US to help afford their lives in America. What does that cost us per year?

The cost per year is $30,000 X 30,000,000 = $900 Billion per year
The cost of deportation is $10,000 X 30 million = $300 Billion one time

The first-year savings is a net of $600 Billion after deportation. The second and subsequent years, the savings would be the full $900 Billion per year

Rather than look at the unpleasant task of coerced deportation, many countries across the world have instituted what they call Pay-to-Go programs in which a free return and a stipend incentive are offered to the migrants to induce them to return home. In our country we would be incenting illegal interlopers living in the shadows of America.

A very nice stipend amount that would persuade many interlopers to return to their home country is $20,000. In this way, the deportation is really a voluntary emigration back to the home country.

The cost of the stipend at $20,000 X 30,000,000 = $600 Billion one time. This is if the country is the USA.

In this example, the cost of the return and the cost of the stipend would be $900 billion if every interloper agreed to return home and then executed on their promise.

This is the same amount as the cost to support all interlopers in the US for one year. The difference between the two is the savings. In year 1, in this scenario, the savings would be zero dollars and the cost would be zero dollars. In year two an annual savings of $900 billion would begin to accrue. Where does the savings come from? It comes from the US not having to pay welfare to illegals as well as Americans being able to get jobs that pay substantially more than when the interlopers were depressing wages by accepting sub-minimum wage positions. .

Suppose the Pay-to-Go stipend were raised to $50,000, to attract more takers, the annual savings of as much as $900 billion would begin to accrue in year three so the stipend could be paid for. After year three, the US is in the black on the program.

Talk to your Congress

I predict that the biggest obstacle in solving the problem of 60 million illegal interlopers in America will be both chambers of the US Congress. I am not naïve enough to suggest that the current Congress' predilection for more voters and lower wages for all Americans could be overcome by the fact that this plan to deal with resident interlopers is the best yet conceived. So, if they remain recalcitrant, we may be forced to replace the entire Congress in order to do the right thing for America.

John McCain is known for his personal estimate of about 4 million per year jumping the border. He is talking about Illegal aliens, which we like to refer to as illegal interlopers. An interloper is another word for an uninvited guest.

McCain's estimate is of those who have chosen to cross the southern border. In his estimate, he does not include the million or more a year who simply decide not to go home when their visas expire. Instead they opt for illegal residency in the US. That's how we got into this problem in the first place. We did not invite 60 million people to America to sponge off US taxpayers. However, some of our elite representatives may very well have done exactly that.

US. amnesty advocate John McCain, is a recognized authority on the subject of illegal immigration. In a letter dated February 2004, he wrote that apprehension figures demonstrated that "almost four million people crossed the US border illegally in 2002."

McCain estimates over 10,000 cross every day. If it were exactly 10,000, then 3,650,000 per year would be his estimate. Instead he simply rounded it up to 4 million. That comes to 128 million from 1986, the year of the Reagan amnesty to the end of 2017. If we cut that in half and round it down, we're looking at my long-time estimate of 60 million interlopers in residence today. I know that nobody can prove me wrong on that number.

...

What about legal immigration?

About 1.2 million green cards are expected to be issued in 2017. In 2014, a total of 1,016,518 persons became lawful permanent residents—aka, LPRs complete with green card status. Over half of the new LPRs (53 percent) already lived in the United States when they were granted lawful permanent residence. Sixty-four percent of the new LPRs were granted lawful permanent resident status based on a family relationship with a U.S. citizen or lawful permanent resident of the United States. The leading countries of birth of new LPRs were Mexico (13 percent), India (7.7 percent), and China (7.5 percent)

The other type of legal resident in the US is known as a birthright citizen, colloquially known as an anchor baby.

If the stipend is a little higher, the Pay-to-Go Program could save the US another ton of funds if it were also used to attract green card holders on welfare, and anchor babies on welfare. When and if they agreed to return to their home countries there would no longer be a cost for their welfare. Think of what the US could do with another half trillion or as much as a full trillion dollars per year to spend on American interests?

The three categories for which the program could be used to include would be the following:
1. Current interlopers
2. Legal green card holders on welfare
3. Anchor babies at any age, including children supervised by a legal or illegal parent.

The recommended stipend for each of the three categories would be as follows:
1. Current Interlopers $20,000
2. Legal Green Card Holders on Welfare $30,000
3. Anchor Babies or Adults $50,000

Anybody opting for a stipend in any of the above categories would be prohibited without special petition from ever returning to the United States for any reason. Any debt accrued that is accounted for in the Accountability system, explained in Chapter 17. would need to be collected prior to any request for readmission to be examined.

There are 15 million legal immigrants (green card holders) currently in the country. Half of them are on welfare. 7.5 million X $30,000 = $225 Billion per year. There are 6 million birthright citizens (former anchor babies) born to illegal aliens currently in the country. They are almost all on welfare 6 million X $30,000 = $180 Billion per year

The US can thus save an additional $405 Billion per year by adding the above two categories to the illegal interlopers able to use the Pay-to Go program or any other program that reduces costs to zero. This would make a total of three categories for which the program could be used.

What problem does the Pay-to Go program fix? It is a pro-America and pro-American citizen solution. It is an America-First solution to the major problem of 60 million illegal residents sponging off the taxpayers in the United States.

Once in the continental US, the interlopers either wholly or partially depend on US taxpayer dollars for their daily sustenance. Is your wallet looking a little thinner these days? The problem we plan to solve in this book, the real problem, is that 60 million illegal foreign nationals cost Americans money every day. They just don't pay their way and live here. They take from US.

Chapter 9 Pay-to-Go

Pay-to-Go

America-First Immigration Fix

Brian W. Kelly

America-First Immigration Fix

Book purpose:

In Chapter 8, Legalizing Illegal Aliens Via Resident Visas, we discussed the purpose of a plan that legalizes illegal aliens who choose to stay in America with conditions that include no vote, no welfare, no citizenship, etc. In the beginning of the chapter, we presented a summary of the plan.

This book, Pay-to-Go, with a plan of the same name, Pay-to-Go, is a companion program to the Resident Visa Plan. It has many of the same purposes. The difference between the two major plans is that under Pay-to-Go, illegal foreign nationals choose not to stay in America. Instead, they go back to their home countries for good. To help them out when they get home, the US provides them full transportation costs plus a stipend from $20,000 to $50,000 depending on their status:

1. Illegal Alien
2. Green Card
3. Anchor Baby.

After a year or so, based on the cost of welfare, and the size of the stipend, the US government under Pay-to-Go will save $30,000 for each person who takes this deal. If everybody took the deal, this would save the US over $500 billion per year. Similar savings are achieved for those who choose to stay in America under the Resident Visa Plan.

Most illegal foreign national live with welfare support

Illegal immigrants living in the shadows use stolen and fake IDs to survive. It is a fact. It is much easier than you would think for those in the hidden economy of the US to gain welfare benefits including healthcare. Hospital social services departments are motivated to sign illegals up for Medicaid rather than absorb the EMTALA (ER) costs themselves. The estimated cost per illegal on welfare is $30,000 per year. That is a lot of money.

The fake news estimate for how many illegals live in America is about 11 million. Donald Trump estimates the number at 30 million. However, if we consider that since 1986, thirty-two years ago, from one to three million per year have crossed our borders without documentation.

That means that by all accounts, we have between 32 million to 96 million foreign interlopers scratching a living from the shadows using fake ids, welfare, and whatever means possible to survive. John McCain has estimated that there are 128 million foreign interlopers in America today. So, for a reality check, let's just say the number is closer to 60 million than 11 million. Yet, our statistics systems are so poor that nobody really knows.

There are estimates that the US welfare agencies at various levels as well as health agencies and school systems spend as much as $500 billion per year taking care of illegal foreigners. Considering that as many as half of the green card holders, who are permanent legal immigrants are on the welfare dole in one way or another. The costs to American taxpayers are staggering.

If we permitted all such residents who wanted to go home to go home all expenses paid, and we gave them $20,000 to as much as $50,000 in the form of a stipend to leave, in as little as one year or as many as three years, the US would have a net gain of as much as $500 billion per year thereafter. It would cost us nothing and after a short while, we would be $500 billion to the good each year.

Of course, not all those eligible would opt to leave so we would need another program such as a Resident Visa Plan, described in another book. To handle those who choose to stay in the country legally and agree not to accept benefits.

When you read this book, you will find that the biggest problem with 60,000,000 interlopers in America is that your friendly representative in Congress does not respect your concerns for America. Americans must send home their representatives as they no longer represent the people.

How is it possible that 60 million illegal aliens are living today in America and Congress is not even talking about it? Well, Congress invited them here as sure as they are seated in the Capitol of the country every day doing nothing to help their constituents.

As difficult as it is for good, hard-working Americans to believe, our government has been working to keep us poor. Former President Obama's de-facto amnesties and a do-nothing Congress made it tough for Americans to find work while competing against these foreign interlopers.

Congress has been lying, and yet their efforts have produced a terrible truth—Americans have been left behind and nobody cares. Meanwhile, uninvited guests, working for peanuts, have reduced wages and taken the few jobs that exist today. After they get here, these poor souls languish in misery and a lifetime of poverty as even what they take from our welfare system is hardly enough.

Pay-to-Go is used in countries all over the world, including Australia, to pay foreign workers or foreign interlopers to go home expenses paid and often with a generous stipend. Pay-to-Go needs to be implemented in America. The plan would be to help Americans-first and it would be designed to help illegal foreign nationals in residence to have a much better life with cash in their pockets in their home countries. With this plan, they will no longer be chained to greedy businesses looking for slave-labor wages.

Those who sign up for the program will have a chance to go home and enjoy life with a huge stipend that actually pays for itself. Not only would it cost Americans nothing after a few years, it would provide a lot of dollars to the treasury. There's lots more! You're going to like this America-first plan built by an American for Americans! Talk to your representative to make sure this plan passes in the Congress.

Preface:

In this book, we provide arguments that 60 million illegal aliens in our one-time All-American Country is a problem for the US to sustain. The arguments are both cultural / social and financial. Analysts have presented the case that the yearly cost for supporting so many foreign nationals on our dime is between $500 billion and $1.5 trillion per year and it is growing each year as interlopers just love our eighty odd welfare programs.

There are so many social programs that even after reviewing them multiple times, even I cannot recite them from memory. Nobody can figure out why we have so many welfare programs. But, the illegal foreign nationals are well versed on them all when they come to live in America. There is much redundancy and many programs could be eliminated or replaced without altering the needs addressed. But that is a topic for another day.

Nonetheless, the foreign interloper of today lives in the shadows and he or she understands enough English to be able to know the welfare regulations in the US. Those interlopers with major English skills become the consiglieri for all others wishing to learn how to game the US welfare system.

If illegal aliens came to America seeking a better life and then chose to work for it and never took the amounts needed to support their lives in America, some Americans would say that was OK— even though their residency came about by them committing a crime. But, they learn early all about how to outfox a bunch of bureaucrats who might as well be wearing signs that say, "outfox me!" and the interlopers go ahead and outfox them.

These big mooches, whoever they are, need to be extricated from our country as soon as possible. We simply cannot afford them. We never could. We are $21 Trillion in debt trying to help the world while our own people are without jobs. We need to help ourselves first. The costs for interloper largesse is unsustainable as you will learn in this book.

This book announces a new program for America that Congress has not yet approved or considered. It is designed to help Americans and interlopers. It is built for Americans-first. However, it is also built to help interlopers escape the yoke of US managers who have them working for slave wages. This program can change their lives for the good, in ways they had never imagined.

I wrote this book to help Americans know what our President and Congress can do to force our government to regain control of our borders, ensure our national security, keep our culture, enforce our laws, protect American jobs, make our language the language of the nation, and keep all Americans from being overwhelmed by illegal foreign nationals who offer few benefits and no allegiance to America.

In addition to showing why amnesty is not the right medicine, I take the time to explain in detail the best plan for America to again become a sovereign state with America-loving Americans in charge.

You are going to love this book as well as the Pay-to-Go plan itself. With this plan, all interlopers will have the opportunity for a great life in their home countries with their complete families.

Illegal foreign nationals should be well pleased because the plan uses deportation as a very last resort and it immediately gets illegal foreign nationals out of the shadows as they await to return home. Few books are a must-read but Pay-to-Go: America-First Immigration Fix will quickly appear at the top of America's most read list. It also has a catchy subtitle. One of the big advantages for good-hearted Americans who are afraid of the pain that coerced deportations might cause the families of interlopers:

No More Deportations from America!!!

Table of Contents

Ch 1 Introduction to Pay-to-Go
A Land of Immigrants

The US for all of its existence, even before the War of
Independence, would be characterized as a migrant receiving
country. From colonial days until now our population went from
a few thousand to 325 million and of course everybody here today
was not born in America. We are truly a land of immigrants.

We currently take in a million to two million legal immigrants per
year and from two-million to four million illegal immigrants aka
foreign interlopers. The interlopers (uninvited "guests") get here
by either crossing our borders without authorization or over
staying legal visas. The four million figure comes from Senator
John McCain, a well-known authority on immigration. The US is
clearly the largest receiver of migrants in the world.

More and more Americans are finding it difficult to make ends
meet in the new "COME ON DOWN" mentality fostered by
government officials. The atmosphere today in America regarding
the border interlopers, makes it seem like we have permanently
positioned Bob Barker at the Border with a big megaphone:
"Come on Down!"

We'll take anybody today in the US, or so it seems. Nobody is checking. On the legal side, we even have a Visa Lottery because visas are so hard to get. 50,000 lucky people from across the world get to come to America for a life supported by American taxpayers.

You are in! You do not have to speak English and in fact, you don't have to speak at all. Say thanks to our corrupt Congress and our greedy businessmen for the lack of rules to protect American citizens.

If you resemble that remark, more than likely, you can thank past President Obama who continually intervened to assure nobody was left behind; nobody was really deported; and there were no restrictions on foreign interlopers taking American jobs—even those that had been in the family for years.

And, yes while simply being employed on a sub-minimum wage scale, our uninvited guests have unwittingly helped millions of greedy businesses lower their normal and customary wage in the country so that it is tough for anybody doing physical labor to make ends meet today.

The US has never used a pay-to-go approach in our history, but it is about time we gave it a try. Our treasury is being overwhelmed by demands from foreigners for more welfare. The cost of interlopers to our economy and our treasury is overwhelming.

Pay-to Go (receiving return transportation costs and a stipend for returning home from a host country such as the US) can even the playing field again and save the US hundreds of billions of dollars to boot.

Unlike America, other immigrant-receiving countries have for decades employed policies to encourage unauthorized immigrants to return to their home countries without the cost, legal barriers, and political obstacles of removals or forced returns—i.e. deportations. The US is a young country and we need to examine closely how others have dealt with excessive immigration and what can be termed pay to stay welfare benefits.

In other countries, nudging an interloper to go back home are a series of noncoercive, pay-to-go, voluntary, assisted voluntary, and non-forced returns. The countries generally offer paid travel and/or other financial incentives such as stipends to encourage unauthorized immigrants to cooperate with immigration officials and leave host countries to return home.

Ch 2 Pay-to-Go Plans in Other Countries
Paying a migrant to return home can work

Time Magazine online tells a story of Nexar Sambrano, who seemed to be living the immigrant dream in Spain. He had come to Barcelona in 2005 after leaving a near-subsistence existence on a farm in Ecuador. Times were good. He found a good-paying delivery job with the local beer company. Unfortunately, things changed.

After 18 months Nexar was doing so well and had tucked enough savings aside that he was hoping to bring his children and his girlfriend over to join him. Out of nowhere, the recession hit, and it affected everybody. Nexar lost his job. He was talented in the trades and was able to get by with odd jobs such a painting or doing masonry. However, it just was not enough.

Time quotes him as saying: "I was relying on my friends for food." So, when the Spanish government offered him money to go home, he took it.

When this Time piece was written it had been over two years since Spain had enacted its Voluntary Return Plan for immigrants, which grants legal residents who lose their jobs the right to receive their entire unemployment benefit in two lump sums — one upon departure, and the second after arriving in their country of origin. This is part of a trend in countries who had once been welcome hosts to migrants when things were good, and they needed extra labor to get the work done.

Over the last several years, some 17,000 documented migrants from the U.S., Eastern Europe, and Africa have signed on to the plan, part of a successful effort, says the government, to reduce the pressure on the Spanish economy and spark development in other parts of the world.

Too many people in a country is not good

The last thing that any country needs, especially as we have yet to fully climb out of The Great Recession is an excess of people. Among other things, they will be demanding to eat and to have a minimum of modest amenities. In the US of course, do-gooders want them all to have colored TV sets, iPads, and other goodies to make their stays comfortable. All of this is very costly to the host country.

Ch 3 Pay-to-Go Programs in History
The US would not be the first Pay-to-Go!

World governments have used voluntary return programs with stipend incentives (Pay-to-Go), and without incentives, long before the recent economic downturn and long before interlopers crossed borders illegally to take advantage of the host country's major benefit packages. Pay-to-Go has served various policy goals beyond coping with economic issues, such as what we are examining in America -- combating illegal immigration, addressing the detention of rejected asylum seekers, migrant over-population reduction, and promoting development through return migration.

For example, France, Germany, Belgium, and the Netherlands experimented with Pay-to-Go programs from the mid-1970s until the mid-1980s due to a poor economic climate, and the infamous 1973-1974 big oil embargo, among other circumstances. These countries sought to provide incentives for both employed and unemployed guest workers to return to their countries of origin. The host countries could not afford to keep them when their own people were not working.

Sixty million illegal foreign interlopers in the US today in a busted economy would not make the situation easier but for sure there would be a lot of takers.

The 2008-2009 Great Recession prompted massive unemployment among the approximately 350,000 Nikkeijin (Latin American workers residing in Japan who at one time emigrated from Japan), residing in Japan. Between November 2008 and January 2009, 9,296 foreigners registered as employment seekers. This was an 11-fold increase from the same period a year earlier.

There have been a number of immigration surveys conducted in Japan. Approximately 40 percent of Latin American workers, most of them Nikkeijin, were unemployed by the end of 2008 and the beginning of 2009, compared to the 5 percent unemployment rate among Brazilians and Peruvians in Japan in 2005.

The recession hit Nikkei (Nikkeijin) workers hardest, as many relied on contract-based employment and jobs that are sensitive to economic fluctuations.

With the economic hardships, massive return migration to Latin America has occurred, primarily due to large-scale layoffs of Nikkei workers and their inability to find new jobs before their unemployment insurance expires.

The point of all this discussion is that Japan uses incentive methods as necessary to move segments of the population to other countries to help its own citizens.

Ch 4 Pay-to-Go Down Under
No coercion necessary

The informal notion of a voluntary return or voluntary repatriation is most simply explained as a migrant, after arriving in a host state willingly deciding (no coercion) that they would like to return home (aka country of origin). More formally, we can say that it is the return of a displaced person, a rejected asylum seeker, a refugee, a victim of trafficking, or a stranded migrant who is unable or unwilling to remain in the host country and who volunteers to return to their country of origin.

There are various programs in different countries to help such people leave and return to their home countries when it is appropriate or simply when they are ready to come back home. The programs are most often built with some level of assistance in the expenses of travel to get home and sometimes they also include a stipend and sometimes they include assistance in the home country for reintegration and resettlement.

In Australia, for example, their AVR program is used as a vehicle to help migrants. It is also used to thin out any overpopulation of migrants who, in times of recession, may very well hold positions that citizens desire. The program helps the return of migrants who have no ongoing legal avenue to stay. However, the program once in effect is generally available to any migrant who needs assistance to return home.

Through small policy changes, Australia had been able to learn from AVR programs in other countries who are suffering similar circumstances with an over population of foreign-born non-citizens. The learning has helped Australia achieve a greater number of returns, thereby reducing the drain on their treasury.

As much as the US is a major magnet for the world's migrants, it is also substantially easier and far less expensive to get to than Australia. Australia might in fact be even more crowded than the US if the migrant population could get there by walking, by motor car or motor coach, or by railroad.

Pay-to-Go AVR programs

All AVR programs are designed to assist migrants to return home. The kind of assistance to a migrant varies from case to case depending on the national policy of a particular host country. The US would do well to follow Australia's lead.

I wrote this book to help Americans know what our President and Congress can do to help force our government to regain control of our borders, ensure our national security, keep our culture, enforce our laws, protect American jobs, make our language the language of the nation, and keep all Americans from being overwhelmed by illegal foreign nationals who offer few benefits and no allegiance to America.

Additionally, it is necessary for illegal foreign nationals to also be very pleased with a solution to their being stranded in our country living in poverty in our shadows. They should be happy with this plan which uses deportation as a very last resort and it immediately gets illegal foreign nationals out of the shadows and onto an all-expenses-paid trip back to their home country with a big wad of sheckles left for pocket change purchases and funding for a great start in their home country.

...

Chapter 10 Obamacare: A One-Line Repeal

Obamacare: A One-Line Repeal
Brian W. Kelly

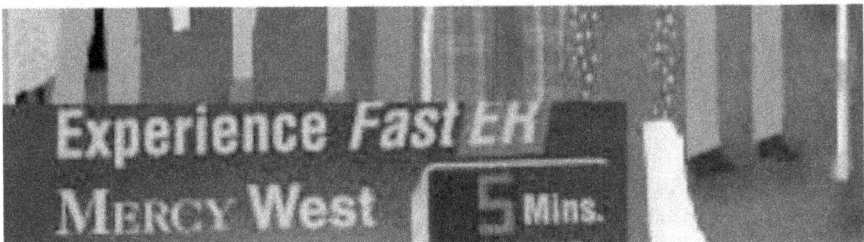

Experience *Fast ER*
MERCY West   5 Mins.

Congress must get this done!

Book purpose:

Most Americans looked at the idea of repeal and replace
Obamacare as a really simple notion. Unfortunately, the *replace*
part was not well understood by the people. It was intentional
chicanery by the government so that Republicans would get credit
for repealing Obamacare while putting back a system that was in
fact Obamacare with just a few changes. Most Americans paying
attention did not like the bait and switch pulled on us by officials
in the Republican Party.

Therefore, we are still looking for a one-line repeal. Just repeal it!
Get it done. None of us, who lost our former healthcare to Obama
chicanery, care about a replacement. Go back to whatever the
laws were in existence when Obamacare became effective. It is
OK if **after** the big repeal, to get some touch up work done such as
keeping kids on policies until they are 26 and some guarantees
about not being dropped by a carrier and something fair about
preexisting conditions. The repeal should be one line and that one
line must take away everything including the death panels.

Polls propping up Obamacare are lies just like Obamacare has always been a lie

Despite what Democrats wanting to make former President
Obama into a modern saint will say; most thinking Americans
hate Obamacare. Why is that? The answer is simple, Americans
have worked for healthcare since the Roosevelt days and they do
not want the government in charge of their healthcare. Yes, it is
that simple, but Congress, who made themselves immune to the
effects of Obamacare does not share their pain.

Americans have a quiet fear as they give up their rights to first-
class healthcare that the guy who gets all the political jobs will be
designated in their neighborhood as the guy who determines
whether they get treatment or not, and what is covered.

Health insurance gained by getting a good job and working hard to keep it no longer will matter. Johnny B. Good, the guy who put up the spite fence next door to you—the guy with the four Pit Bulls, will cup his hands to his face after you make your plea, and then he will decide if your operation is needed. Your money won't matter when Johnny from the Neighborhood is in charge. That thought alone scares Americans to death.

Americans are not happy with Obamacare's increasing premium costs and its increasing out-of-reach deductibles, and they don't like that doctors are dropping out of Obamacare like flies giving thus decreasing access to professionals Americans know what they don't like.

They also know what they do like. They know that they do not want the government, especially neighborhood guys like Johnny B. Good making health decisions for their family. I applaud the efforts of good and honest US representatives willing to put a steel tip on their shoe and boot Obamacare out of town for good.

President Trump intrinsically knows how to do business logically without convoluted rules. The plan outlined right here in this book shows how our wonderful President can use the simplest methodology ever to repeal and replace Obamacare with a market based solution—exactly the way he promised during the campaign.

I predict that you will read this book from cover to cover in one sitting.

Why do people hate Obamacare?

Few people today trust the polls that are continually being reported by both the real and the fake news media. So, when those who hate Obamacare just nose out those who love Obamacare when just 10 million people are on Obamacare out of a country-full, it does not add up. People see a failed program that stinks of politics and government control and unless they get theirs for free, they want it gone and fast.

Most of my friends just roll their eyes at ne mention of the word Obamacare. This is often followed by a bunch of negative phrases.

Though from what I see, it is worse than the polling results, which are not positive for Obamacare. About 40% of Americans held an unfavorable opinion of the law in April 2010, while 46% had a favorable view. This poll was by a Kaiser Family Foundation poll who for whatever reason always report Obamacare in a positive light.

Since the original polling, the public's perception has generally been less positive and recently the numbers are more like 45% of the people having a negative view, versus 43% with a positive one. To me, if this is accurate, it can only be a poll of the uninformed by the biased.

We all know that Donald Trump promised a swift _repeal of Obamacare_ and this helped him win the election. At a swanky New Year's Eve bash at his Mar-a-Lago Club, he drew raucous, extended applause from the black-tie crowd when he recently repeated the vow. Only a dummy wants government in control of healthcare. Johnny B Good would not be good for anybody's healthcare.

One gentleman from Virginia, in a survey recently offered this response:

"It's a welfare program disguised as a health care program," said Charles Kraut, 67, a financial adviser who believes the smaller government is, the better. "Please show me where in the Constitution it says that the government should "promote the general welfare" by stealing from half the population to give to the other half." This gentleman has health insurance through his, but he resents having his tax dollars go things he would never get as options on his health insurance such as sex-change operations and abortions on demand.

Many others say there is nothing affordable about the Affordable Care Act. They resent that they were lied to by the President that premiums would go down and they could choose their own doctors. What they got was high premiums and deductibles that get worse every year. They are also angry that they couldn't keep the insurance plan or doctors that they had. It is not nice for politicians to try to fool the part of the public that pays attention.

Table of Contents

Ch 1 Setting the Table
Congress not interested in Americans or truth

...

After seven years of promising to repeal and replace Obamacare, the verdict is in, at least so far. When Republicans got their chance with a majority in the Senate and the House as well as owning the presidency, they reneged. Their promise to do exactly what they said was a lie of convenience to get elected.

...

Obamacare's repeal is, at least for the foreseeable future, dead. John McCain hates Donald Trump as much as he hates his own word.

The simplest explanation of why the Obamacare effort repeal failed is that McCain's vote — coupled with longstanding opposition from Sens. Lisa Murkowski (R-AK) and Susan Collins (R-ME) — meant that the Health Care Freedom Act could not move through the chamber.

Congress often uses deceit and lies to buffalo the American people. Soon, the buffaloing buffoons will be whistling their way out of their own cozy chairs as the people vote in replacement players. Americans do not like liars.

Ch 2 Ryancare-- No Chance of Becoming Law Silly Congressional rules must be changed

If we ever accept again a premise that Paul Ryan intends to do what is right for the American people, shame on us? Ryan claimed to put out a premise that he had constructed the best bill possible to repeal and replace Obamacare as he and the Republicans promised to the American people? There were just two things wrong with his bill: It neither repealed nor replaced Obamacare. If we can get past that, and we still think Ryan did his well-intentioned best, then he clearly failed.

If on the other hand as some suggest, Ryan's objective was to snooker the American people while snookering President Trump into thinking the only way to pass anything was to pass his elite establishment concoction euphemistically labeled as The American Healthcare Act of 2017, for a while at least, he accomplished his goal.

The bill was replete with so many twists and turns that it was as if Ryan was hoping that with enough wrong turns, it would bring him to the right place. Unfortunately, few of us were convinced he wanted to take us anyplace good nor anyplace he had promised.

The House bill which Paul Ryan pushed to "repeal and replace" Obamacare quickly became a bill that nobody wanted to own. Tell me folks, do any of us think that fact alone demonstrated enough about this legislation?

Donald Trump, God love him for his energy, was erroneously told by Mr. Ryan that what he saw, was all he could get. He was also told that Mr. Ryan as the Speaker of the House could deliver it as it existed in a binary vote in the House. So much wanting something rather than nothing. The President went for it. He believed Ryan to be a truthful man. More and more see that supposition as a mistake!

There was a major problem causing all the stink. The bill did not accomplish the # 1 objective. It did not repeal Obamacare. How can a repeal and replace bill not do the repeal?

Ch 3 The Simple Solution
Need honest representation

I was very impressed with the work of Jim Jordan on the Obamacare repeal that I sent him a note. It included my plan that demonstrates how easy the process can be.

March 8, 2017
Representative Jim Jordan
3121 West Elm Plaza
Lima, Ohio 45805

Dear Congressman Jordon,

Thank you for asking for the legislation promised to all Americans from Republicans regarding the complete repeal of Obamacare. I agree that what is on the table is not what was promised.

I sent a letter to my home paper, which prescribed a simple solution that Americans would like. I suspect your solution is similar. I send this to you in the event it may help. The parts that were printed in the paper are at this URL:

http://citizensvoice.com/opinion/replacing-obamacare-should-be-simple-1.2163103

The parts that were not printed show that Obamacare affects just 4% of the population. Why we are doing handstands on legislation that can be straightforward is a conundrum for me unless Washington wants to retain control of our healthcare. The entire letter, as sent to the editor, is shown below

Repealing and Replacing Obamacare Should Be Simple:

First of all, the nastiest part of Obamacare is its 20,000+ pages which include the 2700 pages in the legislation and in total about

20,000 pages of regulations. US citizens need to have this onerous burden lifted from our backs.

When we consider that after 7 years, just 4% of the population is "benefiting" from Obamacare, it makes it look like a silly experiment in government buffoonery. The KISS approach should apply here (Keep It Simple, Stupid!).

Why it is taking so long to come up with a solution means government must be trying to keep control. Government should have little to no control and should make a graceful exit from running and controlling American healthcare.

Here are some facts:

Citizen population of the US is now 325 million

- 45 million get insurance from Medicare
- 70 million get insurance from Medicaid and CHIP
- 152 million get insurance from employers
- 13 million get insurance from Obamacare exchanges
- 60 million are either other-insured, self-insured or uninsured.

Under Obamacare, firms with 100 or more full-time equivalent employees (FTE) needed to insure at least 70% of their full-time workers by 2015 and 95% by 2016.

Those with 50 or less employees do not have to pay for employees' insurance. In 2015, 56% of non-elderly residents (270M *.56 = 152M) got their health insurance through work.
About 87% of the 13 million who buy Obamacare through Exchanges are getting some form of cost assistance to cover premiums and deductibles.

Costs and deductibles for those getting no subsistence are huge and unaffordable. For example, Mrs. X, a 63-year old real person recently compared prices for individual health insurance plans and can't believe what she found:

"They cost $1,200 a month, and they have a deductible of $6,000," she said. "I don't know how they think anyone can afford that." Mrs. X lives in Hull, Georgia,

Though it is only 13 million of 325 million right now who are under Obamacare, many citizens fear the government control that comes with Obamacare and its high premiums, poor access, and huge deductibles. Mrs. X will pay over $20,000 before Obamacare buys her a single aspirin.

The 87% who receive cost subsidies when surveyed, report that they are very pleased with Obamacare. This is understandable but not representative of the full population. After all, the rest of us are paying for their subsidies.

Millions like Mrs. X have realized they are too poor for Obamacare. There are lots of reasons why it is so expensive such as silly things like Mrs. X at 63 needs pre-natal care to be included in her policy. Moreover, Mrs. X can only buy insurance from somebody licensed in her state. v

The solution is very simple but just like it took 7 years for President Obama to get us to this point of crisis, it is not an overnight solution. However, with immediate action, the solution can begin immediately. I mean like tomorrow. I would project that in 2 to 2.5 years we can be 100% rid of Obamacare control of healthcare.

Here are the ingredients

1. Repeal Obamacare immediately [Use a one-line repeal] rendering the 2700 original pages of government control, with added regulations reaching 20,000 pages (three feet of paper) obsolete.

2. Begin the transition to a market-based system in two years. No citizens should be harmed during this process. The market system would have no government involvement and non-Obamacare polices, such as those from before 2010; should begin to be written immediately. The changes would include:

A. Permit insurance companies to immediately sell across state lines any policy that provides marketplace healthcare insurance to any potential subscriber. Make it so Obamacare policies may be canceled by the insured at any time during the two-year transition period if desired. No more new Obamacare policies will be issued.

B. Begin a two-year delay before all Obamacare policies are canceled. During this period, all existing healthcare insurance may stay in effect with no more than a 5% per annum increase for those that choose not to change at all. Once the move to a market solution is made by an individual or employer, the two-year hiatus for them is complete.

During the two years, the provision for children on parents' policies and the preexisting conditions stay in effect. Other good rules regarding policy cancellation also continue.

During this two-year period and no longer, the government may have to subsidize this to make up for the past ills of Obamacare. The government made a big mistake and it is proper that it pay for its mistake until the two-years is up.

C. Those who today receive subsidies for Obamacare, may keep them for the two years. Then, their cases are turned over to the states, and they may receive Medicaid if they qualify.

D. When the two-year wait is up, Medicaid control goes back to the States.

E. When Obamacare is gone in two years. these are the options: Medicare; Medicaid and Chip; Insurance from employer; Private insurance; other-insurance, self-insurance or no insurance.

Sincerely,

Brian W. Kelly

I think that about does it but here is one more thought:

What do the people want?

A one-line repeal bill is all that is needed and then let the Marketplace takeover with a few well-meaning tweaks if necessary. But, just a few!

I am not the first to suggest a very short bill. But, I am the first to suggest a one-line bill.

A great one sentence bill

On March 28, 2017 as reported by Fox News, an Alabama congressman introduced a one-sentence bill in the House Friday to repeal Obamacare. I love that my recommended bill size is smaller, but I am more tickled that there are others that think the charade of repeal and replace has gone on too long. Just repeal.

Let the marketplace replace it!

Mo Brooks has become one of my living heroes

Republican Representative Mo Brooks from Alabama, introduced the bill as the Obamacare Repeal Act.

AL.com reported the big sentence:

"Effective as of Dec. 31, 2017, the Patient Protection and Affordable Care Act is repealed, and the provisions of law amended or repealed by such Act are restored or revived as if such Act had not been enacted," The following text would be my one-line repeal:

Obamacare repealed immediately. Specifics to follow.

Don't you just love the tone?

Brooks introduced the bill after he announced that he was against Ryan care, which in its early incarnation, was pulled from a House floor vote because it did not have enough support to pass.

"If the American people want to repeal Obamacare, this is their last, best chance during the 115th Congress," Brooks said in a statement. Those Congressmen who are sincere about repealing Obamacare may prove it by signing the discharge petition..."

"At a minimum, the discharge petition will, like the sun burning away the fog, show American voters who really wants to repeal Obamacare and who merely acts that way during election time."

The bill was not voted on as Paul Ryan considered it a symbolic gesture. Isn't that reflective of why there is little trust in our Congress, especially its leadership.

Mo Brooks constructed and presented a great bill which would not have been a symbolic gesture if Congress wanted to assure that it kept its promise to repeal and replace Obamacare. They could have passed it.

The replace part was implicit as once Obamacare was repealed, insurance companies from all over the world would be flocking like buzzards to the US with the most innovative policies you have ever seen since the beginning of Obamacare.

By the way, though I like my one-line repeal, I would go with Mo Brooks one sentence repeal as it does the same thing.

Chapter 11 60-Million Illegal Aliens in America!!!

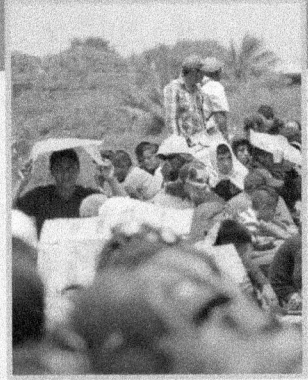

60 MILLION
ILLEGAL ALIENS
IN AMERICA!!!
A simple, America-
first solution

Brian W. Kelly

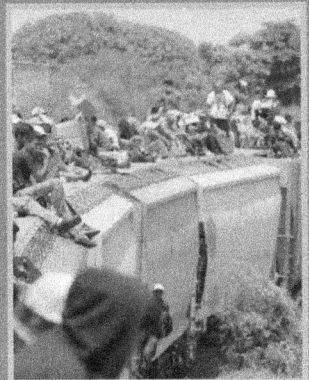

A simple, America-first solution.

Book purpose:

This book is a 2017 predecessor to books already examined titled, *Pay to Go* and *Legalizing Illegal Aliens via Resident Visas*. In this book, the **Pay-to-Go Plan** as originally conceived was called **The Stipend Return Plan.** It was just about the same as *Pay-to-Go. In* conjunction with the *Resident Visa*, the total plan revealed first in this book, solves the problem of 60 million illegal interlopers resident in America.

Donald Trump is on America's side

Donald Trump's signature issue from the announcement of his presidential candidacy has been immigration reform because he loves America and Americans. Trump of course has been focused in preventing entry for intruders by building a big beautiful wall, whereas this book deals head-on with the problem of 60 million resident illegal aliens. Both notions should be part of the administration's immigration strategy.

As difficult as it is for good, hard-working Americans to believe, our government has been working to keep us poor. Former President Obama's de-facto amnesties and a do-nothing Congress made it tough for Americans to find work while competing against foreign interlopers whose minimal wage demands gave them the advantage in the jobs marketplace.

Congress has been laying low and lying when necessary. Unfortunately, their efforts have produced a terrible truth— Americans have been left behind and nobody cares. Meanwhile, uninvited guests, working for peanuts, have reduced wages and taken the few jobs that exist today. After they get here, these poor souls languish in misery and a lifetime of poverty as even what they take from our welfare system is hardly enough to keep them going.

Reviewers of this two-part plan can see that the Resident Visa Plan will help Americans first and that it is also designed to help illegal foreign nationals in have a better life also. They will no longer be chained to greedy businesses looking for slave-labor wages.

The Resident Visa Plan takes interlopers out of the shadows and gives them opportunity. If well-behaved, they gain the right to stay and work in America for a lifetime, one year at a time. They will be out of the shadows with no amnesty, no citizenship, no freebies, no line jumping; and no jobs before Americans. The Stipend-Return Plan will provide a nice dollar bonus to any illegal alien that wants a free trip home with money in their pocket. In a subsequent book, shown previously, we call this Pay-to-Go.

These US immigration goals are satisfied in the Resident Visa Plan and for those who would rather a jump start back in their home country, the Stipend Return plan puts money in their pockets as soon as they arrive in their home country. These two plans are destined to save America a half-Trillion dollars each year.

Those who sign up for the program that permits them to stay in America, must be vetted every year and must pay a fee each year or be deported. There's lots more! You're going to like this America-first plan built by an American for Americans.

Preface:

What would you call a plan that solved a problem for America that most of the Congress seems to have no interest in solving? I have called it many things while perfecting this book, but now let me settle with what I would like to call **The Stipend Return / Resident Visa Plan**.

I had called the plan many things but never hit the nail on the head. This is my vision for a secret sauce solution to fix the problem of 60 million interlopers waking up in America every day. Yes—build the wall, please! But simultaneously solve the residence problem of so many people who do not belong here. Do we really need up to 60 million interlopers in residence? I do not think so. Hey, John McCain thinks there are over 128 million interlopers in residence.

There are many problems with illegal immigration. For the United States, the biggest problem is the fact that the cost of welfare, cash payments, and medical assistance is bankrupting the country. We cannot afford the huge cost that illegal interlopers place on our system when most of them, because of their reliance on identity theft and mad-up fake ID's, collect some form of welfare.

Every resident feels about a $1500 burden from the generous plans that help illegal residents survive in America's shadows. Additionally, wages for Americans are always going down while expenses are going up. The new Stipend Return / Resident Visa program solves both of these problems at the same time.

I am happy that you are reading this book and I hope many others find it and convince the Administration and the Congress and the President that it is their turn to learn about The Resident Visa Plan.

This book is the result of over ten years of work from way back when I wrote my first patriotic book in 2006 titled Taxation without Representation. The 4th edition is now current. The Resident Visa Plan was formalized in 2013 under a different title.

At the time that this work evolved to its current shape, I had examined everything out there especially the Gang of Eight Plan (GO8), existing law, and other notions about how anybody might possibly solve the nation's concerns about 60 million illegal residents.

At first look, I found no real solutions other than either amnesty or follow the law with deportation. The Resident Visa solution is unique, and everything needed to implement it is already in place.

The Resident Visa solution directly addresses the issues that having 60 million illegal foreign nationals in residence have brought upon America. The Gang of Eight approach rewards illegal activity and makes everybody OK and is a bad example, and another approach gives most people a bad, sinking feeling in their gut. That's why nobody has come forward to suggest that 100% deportations are really a good idea for the country. Americans have big hearts.

Deportation is fair of course as these folks have broken our laws. But, our politicians are culpable as they made it too easy for foreigners to break our laws. Amnesty is not a solution as Americans have already paid a big price for the largesse of politicians wanting low wages and those wanting the future votes of today's interlopers.

Ideally, the solution would be to go poof, and every foreign interloper would be taken back to where and when they crossed the border years and years ago. Where is a used Star-Trek Transporter when we need one? This time, however, they would not be re-admitted if they tried to cross.

The raw facts say that the problem never should have reached the level of severity that it is today. Nobody can perform miracles and tricorders and transporters are not invented yet so when we have the closest ingenious thought to a miracle as a solution, we should examine it and embrace it. It is this plan. Doing nothing makes it worse.

After defining the problem in my early books, I developed a methodology that would make Americans pleased and would remove all interlopers from the shadows—and into the light of the American day or back home with some cash in their pockets if they choose.

Americans in this system would have priority and for their right to participate, interlopers would agree to pay their own way while in our country. Such a plan ought to work. Only the bad guys would be deported.

When I carefully read the Gang of Eight "comprehensive" plan in 2013, I noticed that it smelled a lot like it was purposely designed to kill America. No jobs would be left for Americans. Newly unemployed Americans would have to pay for newly minted citizens getting a lifetime of freebies. We would see them voting in national elections; and watch their numbers grow until there were 33 million more foreign nationals looking for jobs by plan—jobs that Americans cannot even find.

Per Heritage.org, the cost for the 33 million that were intended to be brought in by reunification provisions of the Gang of 8 Bill, was estimated at well over $6 Trillion. Even Donald Trump does not have that much money. I think. The bottom line is that this was a terrible deal for the country.

I was hunting for a real immigration fix that pleased Americans. Marco Rubio, Chuck Schumer and the rest of the Gang of Eight were looking for scalps to prove to Democrats that they had the progressive agenda in the forefront. Let me tell you now folks. I do not. Like they did in the 1920's, progressives are again trying to undermine America.

I looked at all the things that Americans want in a real plan— things they liked and things they do not like. I wanted interlopers to embrace the plan, so they could get out of the shadows without hurting Americans. So, among other things, I examined what interlopers liked about living in America.

In my first cut at solving the problem in 2013, I figured out a way to permit well-behaved interlopers to stay in America one year at a time with a realistic annual renewal fee, while giving Americans priority in all ways. It was a good plan but not as perfect as I had hoped. The biggest problem with the plan was that it was difficult to explain in clear concise terms.

I was convinced that the plan actually would work and that it would solve the problem for the long haul and take a huge financial burden off the backs of Americans. And, so, I kept at it, continually improving it until it was perfected.

Every plan requires fine tuning and we would expect this to continue to be the case with the Resident Visa Plan. By implementing the current iteration of the plan, the long-sought solution to the result of illegal immigration is around the corner.

To see what US officials on the pro-American side of the issue would think about such a plan for America, I contacted Pennsylvania Congressman, Lou Barletta. Many know Lou Barletta as a tireless advocate for fighting illegal immigration and amnesty. He is running for the Senate against a very poor legislator, Bob Casey, Jr., in my state of Pennsylvania. I presented a detailed PowerPoint of my ideas in late January 2015 to the Congressman and his chief aid at the time, Joseph Gerdes. After perfecting the plan even more, I reached out again and presented again in 2016 to the Congressman. I am scheduled for another meeting soon.

The Congressman was most pleased with my presentation and the detail that backed up each and every point of the presentation. The Congressman and I continued to engage in a lengthy dialogue on these issues. We spoke about the difficulties in getting immigration legislation for Americans through the House and the Senate, and he updated me as to where the Congress was with some new initiatives in securing the border.

During this interchange, the Congressman helped me understand what was really happening in Washington. For my part, I helped the Congressman to fully understand the benefits of this immigration fix for as many as 60 million foreign nationals residing illegally in America.

Both Congressman Barletta and President Trump have made the wall and border security their # 1 priorities. This plan addresses those interlopers who are already here. We need to protect the border and handle the 60 million interlopers at the same time for the good of America.

My strong recommendation to Congressman Barletta and President Trump is that we add this immigration fix, which I call "The Resident Visa Plan," to the "Beautiful Wall" and the Bills and the Amendments on Border Security. This would be the best anybody could do to solve the problem of resident interlopers in America once and for all.

This would be the first comprehensive and comprehensible immigration plan ever put forward that favored America and Americans over foreign nationals. It is America-First.

I sent the Congressman a text version of the presentation with its new logical flow so that he could take it, read it, and share it without having to figure out the hidden messages within the bullets of a PowerPoint. This new update and the updates in the two books subsequent to this will be in Senator Barletta's hands at the same time that they are on the street for sale.

As I examined the document that I produced that comprises this book, I realized that it was much more complete than the original

Kelly Plan. Its sequencing is much better; and the additions from the Barletta presentation / interview add a lot of missing pieces to the package. And, so, I decided to re-work the text document to make it even better.

In 2013, Americans rejected the Gang of Eight Amnesty Bill. So, here I am again, in my 129th book writing again about the problem of 60 million interlopers making it tough for Americans. This time, however, it is far more simplified and easier to implement.

A key element of this plan is that each year the clock resets on foreign nationals who are permitted here under the Resident Visa Plan. This book, thus focuses on interlopers signing up to become Resident Visa Holders with appropriate renewal assurances for good behavior.

This is **the** tool to accomplish the goal of an America and American-First solution to 60 million interlopers. There are a lot of other adjunct notions besides the Resident Visa Plan such as a solution for visa over stayers, green card holders, as well as a unique solution for current birthright citizens.

The solution for the illegal interloper issue is large enough to warrant its own book. President Trump already has a team of people working on other solutions in the immigration umbrella such as border security and the wall, visa overstays, sanctuary cities and other issues not directly related to the 60 million interlopers taking from Americans every day.

You won't believe how easy the problem of 60 million interlopers is to solve if we can get our legislators to take action or President Trump finds he can take Executive Action.

In summary, this book presents the Resident Visa Plan as the fix and the Stipend Return Plan as a backup fix. Then it offers many other points on why this is the one and only fix to create an America without shadows that favors Americans 100%. There is so much good left over that good-willed interlopers have a lot to gain simply by signing up.

I wrote this book to help Americans know what our President and Congress can do to force our government to regain control of our borders, ensure our national security, keep our culture, enforce our laws, protect American jobs, make our language the language of the nation, and keep all Americans from being overwhelmed by illegal foreign nationals who offer few benefits and no allegiance to America.

In addition to showing why amnesty is not the right medicine, I take the time to explain in detail the best plan for America to again become a sovereign state with America-loving Americans in charge.

You are going to love this book as well as the plan itself. All interlopers immediately are to be registered and accountable. You will see that The Resident Visa Plan (SR/RV) is designed by an American for Americans.

Additionally, illegal foreign nationals will be very pleased because the plan uses deportation as a very last resort and it immediately gets illegal foreign nationals out of the shadows. Few books are a must-read but 60 Million Illegal Aliens in America Is a Big Problem will quickly appear at the top of America's most read list. It also has a catchy subtitle:

This is a simple, America-first solution if Congress and the President have the guts! It solves the problem!

Table of Contents

Ch 1 The CliffsNotes Version
60 million interlopers in 60 seconds

I do not have to go far out on a limb to suggest that if we knew how to immediately stop the drain on our government treasuries with one bold and very fair move, our representatives would be forced to adopt the measures necessary to achieve the gains. In this case, it would be to stop the major treasury drain that occurs each and every day to support a population segment of illegal interlopers. The term interloper, whether legal or illegal, means *uninvited guest*.

Based on what it costs to support illegal foreign nationals. we can certainly afford to deport millions of people. However, there are many good reasons why we should not deport anybody other than criminals. Most of the 60 million illegal residents are hardworking and living quiet, orderly lives. We also cannot allow them, as a result of their illegal entry, to become citizens. This would violate the basic premise of following the rule of law that is a key standard of citizenship. This book offers two great solutions to solve this big problem.

By the way, in this abbreviated "CliffsNotes" chapter, we net it out, so it can be well understood. I predict that the biggest obstacle in solving the problem of 60 million illegal interlopers in America will be both chambers of the US Congress. I am not naïve enough to suggest that the current Congress' predilection for more voters and lower wages for all Americans could be overcome by the fact that this plan to deal with resident interlopers is the best yet conceived. So, we may be forced to replace them all (Congress) in order to do the right thing for America.

We cannot let our corrupt Congress get in the way of our solving our problem with the 60 million. I admit that this would probably be more difficult than stopping the treasury loss but at least we would all know what we must do, and seeing Congress packing would be a pleasure to the senses.

John McCain is known for his estimate of a clip of about 4 million per year. Illegal aliens (interlopers) have chosen to cross the southern border or they have chosen to simply overstay their visas in order to gain residence in the US. Amnesty advocate John McCain, who is a recognized authority on the subject of illegal immigration, in a letter dated February 2004, wrote that apprehension figures demonstrated that "almost four million people crossed the US border illegally in 2002."

McCain estimates over 10,000 cross every day. Adding it up, that comes to 128 million by the end of 2017. If we cut that in half and round it down, we're looking at my estimate of 60 million interlopers in residence today. I know that nobody can prove me wrong.

The name of the plan to solve the problem of 60 million interlopers makes sense when you think about it. It is the *Stipend Return / Resident Visa Plan*. The little slash means *or* in this case. The program immediately takes 60 million illegal foreign nationals out of the shadows and saves the US treasury a minimum of a half-Trillion dollars each year after year 1. Should Congress and /or the President pursue this plan? Of course!

What problem does the program fix? It is a pro-America and pro-American citizen solution. It is an America-First solution to the major problem of 60 million illegal residents sponging off the taxpayers in the United States. Once in the continental US, the interlopers either wholly or partially depend on US taxpayer dollars for their daily sustenance. Is your wallet looking a little thinner these days? The problem we plan to solve in this book, *the real problem,* is that 60 million illegal foreign nationals cost Americans money every day. They just don't pay their way and live here. They take from US.

...

What if interlopers do not want to go home

If a resident illegal foreign national really does not want to go home regardless of the incentive, then there is another option that actually costs taxpayers nothing and permits the interloper to stay in America indefinitely in a legal state as long as they "behave."

The program provides for granting interlopers in good standing what we are about to call a Resident Visa. This is a new visa type that, unlike other visa types can be renewed each and every year with conditions.

With this, former foreign nationals would be legal under the protection of the Resident Visa and could remain in America as long as they behave in a lawful manner according to the exact terms of their visa.

There are many differences between illegally gaining benefits in the United States and becoming legal by gaining a Resident Visa. Those choosing to employ the Resident Visa to stay in America, are welcome to do so; but the terms of the relationship with US officials will not be the same as when they were illegal.

For example, there would be no more cash incentives. The former interloper would be temporarily legalized after applying for a special US passport and then a Resident Visa and after being approved for both. The visa will be special in that it will be renewable with a fee of $100 required annually after a renewal application, a record update (demographics, etc.), and a re-vetting of the applicant, and a special oath of allegiance.

Why should an illegal alien residing in America in the shadows find either of these two different plans acceptable?

- ✓ Stipend-Assisted Return Program
- ✓ Resident Visa Program

1. No more living in the shadows of America.
2. Opportunity to go home travel-free if desired with a big stipend paid by Americans.
3. US will budget $15 Billion for safe cities in home countries for returning immigrants
4. US will develop 15 safe settlements / cities with 10 in Mexico
5. Can get in line (back of line) in home country for citizenship without leaving US.
6. With renewals, the opportunity to live in America a lifetime.
7. Can obtain a driver's license, insurance, etc.

8. Can keep any job that is already held.
9. Can apply for any job available in America.
10. Can live wherever they want in America.
11. Can get same paid by patient medical insurance as Americans.
12. Can get installment loans from US Government on an exception basis to help with medical and educational expenses. Must be paid back.
13. After five years but no more, living with a Resident Visa, can still opt for stipend to go home.
14. Anchor family stipends to go home are huge ($50,000 per birthright citizen) and cumulative with a no-return promise.

I would suspect that list above provides a lot more advantages for interlopers than most would ever believe from how the corrupt US press will preview this program. Yet, this is just one of two major options that under the Stipend Return / Resident Visa Program, from which illegal residents may choose.

Many of the advantages for current interlopers are listed in the fourteen points above. The first plan provides a pay-to-go option that is more generous than any other country in the world. The second plan is the Resident Visa Program since getting a Resident Visa is all that is needed to win the illegal alien game. If you want to win and stay in America, this is the plan for you.

Winning the illegal alien game thankfully does not mean that Americans are shut out. Any illegal foreign national who opts for the stipend deal and departs for home under the Stipend-Assisted Return Program should have no regrets as all expenses are paid and the stipend is nice, and it includes $20,000 for each alien dependent who are also in the program. A three-child family can provide a $100,000 stipend for the family in the home country and the US can more than afford to pay it.

Knowing this is so beneficial to interlopers, why should Joe America want this program? In a nutshell, it is because Joe America is smart and knows this will save a ton of dollars for him and all Americans.

Many Americans do not trust the government, period. So, why would Americans think this is a good deal if the illegal foreign national does not choose to exit America with a stipend? Then what?

If an illegal foreign national chooses not to accept this US government act of kindness, and does not go home, and does not sign up for The Resident Visa Program—the only two options in the Stipend Return / Resident Visa Program, there is only one course of action left for the government. The interloper will be asked to leave the country at their own expense. They will be deported otherwise.

By the enactment of this new visa and this new "return home" plan, the idea of residing in America in an illegal alien status is being eliminated, period. The lack of a decision by an illegal interloper to choose one or the other will unfortunately provoke immigration authorities to deport them.

Why should an American citizen like these two plans?

1. The days of the free lunch are over.
2. Fee based passport & Resident Visa is designed to be cost free to Americans
3. Return Home stipends pay for themselves in one year
4. Illegal aliens must agree to terms of Resident Visa-- all benefits eliminated after 1st year.
5. Once an illegal alien returns home, cannot come back; no cost is accrued after year 1
6. No birthright citizenship for illegals, permanent residents, and Resident Visa Holders
7. No cash, medical services, education, welfare, or other benefits permitted for those with a Resident Visa.
8. No citizen-only privileges permitted
9. Resident Visa Holders have no right to vote in any election
10. New jobs must go to American citizens first—all things being equal.
11. Fees, fines on employers will help pay for Resident Visa program kickoff. Will generate approximately $400 Billion.
12. When program in high gear, US will save more than $500 Billion per year on interloper expenses.
13. Resident Visa holder must be employed (1 yr. to get a job)

14. Resident Visa holder must have self-paid or employer-paid healthcare
15. Resident Visa holder must pass English test in two years
16. Resident Visa holder must take oath of allegiance to be approved for 1ˢᵗ renewal
17. No more green cards for family reunification-instead use Resident Visa.
18. All green card permanent residence visas are eliminated when expired. No new green cards. Use Resident Visa.
19. Next 10-yr green card renewal becomes a Resident Visa
20. No path to citizenship without going home to get in line (begin a process like all others from that country)
21. Citizenship line -- jumping the line is not permitted.
22. Major cost savings for America

The end of Sanctuary Cities

Victor David Hanson writes: "Sanctuary cities protect illegal aliens from federal immigration agencies in a way that is not true of American citizens who arrive at airports and must go through customs, with no exemption from federal agents examining their passports and personal histories. If crimes or infractions are found, there is no safe space at an airport exempt from federal enforcement."

The SR/RV program either pays illegal interlopers to go or it provides a Resident Visa that offers many benefits to both interlopers and American citizens. For example, it saves about $500,000,000,000 per year after year one of its implementation. With no more illegal aliens in the country, a major advantage is that the divisive notion of Sanctuary Cities and the term Sanctuary Cities can be removed from the US vocabulary. There will be no need for them with residents all being legal.

Anchor babies qualify

The Stipend Return program is also available to those who became citizens through the anchor baby loophole of the 14ᵗʰ amendment. When an Anchor child with parent chooses to join the Stipend Return program, each anchor citizen child will receive a $50,000 stipend and each of his or her interloper parents will receive their own $20,000 for a total of $70,000 for a two-person family and $90,000 for a three-person family with one child. A family of four anchor children with a mom or dad would receive $240,000. With mom and dad, the sum would be $240,000. This is very affordable for US citizens considering the lifetime cost of one anchor baby can be as much as $2 million or more.

DACA "children" also qualify

The SRRV program solves the problem for DACA children also. DACA children qualify for the full $20,000 stipend in the Stipend Return Program. Those in the DACA program also qualify for the Resident Visa Program if they want to stay in the US. As an additional DACA concession for the "Children" who opt for the Resident Visa, there will be no charge for the visa for the first five renewal years. DACA "children" will be vetted when they apply for a resident passport. Gang members, of course, will be deported without benefits.

The evidence is on the table.

Nobody in their right mind wants life to continue with a shadow population who in many ways have been victimized similar to how slaves were victimized many years ago. The Stipend Return and the Resident Visa are programs that provide a way out of the mess for both interlopers and regular Americans.

Greedy fat cat business persons and politicians at the highest levels created this mess for both factions. Consequently, the plan includes substantial fees and fines for those businesses who hired illegal interlopers instead of Americans. Being greedy will cost the fat cats over $400 Billion and perhaps more.

They made a ton of money off the backs of Americans with lower wages while poor interlopers were living in squalor with sub-minimum wages. American industry as represented by the Chamber of Commerce should show some remorse and voluntarily chip in to help solve this problem and back the Stipend Return / Residence Visa Plan as it is a winner for all decent Americans and the long-suffering communities whose only solace is the shadows of America.

Quick Comparison with the Gang of Eight

In 2013, eight US Senators known as the Gang of Eight got a bill passed in the Senate that sold Americans down the river and would have given a ton of benefits to illegal aliens at taxpayer cost. The Stipend Return / Resident Visa Program is pro-American and saves taxpayers substantial dollars. It is nothing like the John McCain / Marco Rubio Gof8 sellout. It is explained in detail later in the book. For now, the following quick comparison chart is shown to help us better understand the new combined program by comparing it in the chart below with the Gang of Eight Program

2013 Gang of Eight v Resident Visa

	G of 8	SR/RV
Border secure	No	More technology
Jobs	Favors Interlopers	Favors Americans
Amnesty	Yes	No
Path to citizenship	Yes	No (almost same as today)
Permanent residents	Yes	Never, renewable visa
Voting	Yes	No, Never
Welfare benefits	Yes	No, Never
Freebies	Yes	No, Never
Anchor babies	Yes	No, stipends to depart
Employer fees/fines	No	Yes -if one illegal employee
Reunification	33M in 10yrs	Not Resident Visa Holders
Coerced-deportation	None	As needed for violations
Return to home country	No	Yes, with stipend
Must have healthcare	No	Yes
Must be employed	No	Yes
Must speak English in 2 yrs?	No	Yes
Oath of allegiance	No	Yes, after 1 year
Cost/debt accountability	No	Yes
Taxpayer Costs	$ 6Trillion	Zero
Payback plan	No	Yes
Accountability Database	No	Yes
Interloper fine	Yes	Yes
Employer fine	No	Yes (helps finance program)
Back taxes	No	Yes (vetting interviews)

Other books by Brian Kelly: (amazon.com, and Kindle)

Boost Social Security Now! Hey Buddy Can You Spare a Dime?
The Birth of American Football. From the first college game in 1869 to the last Super Bowl
Obamacare: A One-Line Repeal Congress must get this done.
A Wilkes-Barre Christmas Story A wonderful town makes Christmas all the better
A Boy, A Bike, A Train, and a Christmas Miracle A Christmas story that will melt your heart
Pay-to-Go   America-First Immigration Fix
Legalizing Illegal Aliens Via Resident Visas Americans-first plan saves $Trillions. Learn how!
60 Million Illegal Aliens in America!!! A simple, America-first solution.
The Bill of Rights By Founder James Madison Refresh *your knowledge of the specific rights for all*
Great Players in Army Football Great Army Football played by great players..
Great Coaches in Army Football Army's coaches are all great.
Great Moments in Army Football Army Football at its best.
Great Moments in Florida Gators Football Gators Football from the start. This is the book.
Great Moments in Clemson Football CU Football at its best. This is the book.
Great Moments in Florida Gators Football Gators Football from the start. This is the book.
The Constitution Companion. A Guide to Reading and Comprehending the Constitution
The Constitution by Hamilton, Jefferson, & Madison – Big type and in English
PATERNO: The Dark Days After Win # 409. Sky began to fall within days of win # 409.
JoePa 409 Victories: Say No More! Winningest Division I-A football coach ever
American College Football: The Beginning From before day one football was played.
Great Coaches in Alabama Football Challenging the coaches of every other program!
Great Coaches in Penn State Football the Best Coaches in PSU's football program
Great Players in Penn State Football The best players in PSU's football program
Great Players in Notre Dame Football The best players in ND's football program
Great Coaches in Notre Dame Football The best coaches in any football program
Great Players in Alabama Football from Quarterbacks to offensive Linemen Greats!
Great Moments in Alabama Football AU Football from the start. This is the book.
Great Moments in Penn State Football PSU Football, start--games, coaches, players,
Great Moments in Notre Dame Football ND Football, start, games, coaches, players
Cross Country With the Parents A great trip from East Coast to West with the kids
Seniors, Social Security & the Minimum Wage. Things seniors need to know.
How to Write Your First Book and Publish It with CreateSpace
The US Immigration Fix--It's all in here. Finally, an answer.
I had a Dream IBM Could be #1 Again The title is self-explanatory
WineDiets.Com Presents The Wine Diet Learn how to lose weight while having fun.
Wilkes-Barre, PA; Return to Glory Wilkes-Barre City's return to glory
Geoffrey Parsons' Epoch... The Land of Fair Play Better than the original.
The Bill of Rights 4 Dummmies! This is the best book to learn about your rights.
Sol Bloom's Epoch ...Story of the Constitution The best book to learn the Constitution
America 4 Dummmies! All Americans should read to learn about this great country.
The Electoral College 4 Dummmies! How does it really work?
The All-Everything Machine Story about IBM's finest computer server.
ThankYou IBM! This book explains how IBM was beaten in the computer marketplace by neophytes

Brian has written 146 books in total. Other books can be found at amazon.com/author/brianwkelly

www.ingramcontent.com/pod-product-compliance
Lightning Source LLC
Chambersburg PA
CBHW070758290326
41931CB00011BA/2061